At Issue

Will the World Run Out of Fresh Water?

Other Books in the At Issue series:

Antidepressants

Are Conspiracy Theories Valid?

Are Privacy Rights Being Violated?

Child Labor and Sweatshops

Child Sexual Abuse

Creationism Versus Evolution

Does Advertising Promote Substance Abuse?

Does Outsourcing Harm America?

Does the World Hate the United States?

Do Nuclear Weapons Pose a Serious Threat?

Drug Testing

The Ethics of Capital Punishment

The Ethics of Genetic Engineering

The Ethics of Human Cloning

Gay and Lesbian Families

Gay Marriage

Gene Therapy

How Can Domestic Violence Be Prevented?

How Does Religion Influence Politics?

Hurricane Katrina

Is American Society Too Materialistic?

Is Poverty a Serious Threat?

Legalizing Drugs

Responding to the AIDS Epidemic

Steroids

What Causes Addiction?

At Issue

Will the World Run Out of Fresh Water?

Debra A. Miller, Book Editor

GREENHAVEN PRESS

An imprint of Thomson Gale, a part of The Thomson Corporation

Detroit • New York • San Francisco • New Haven, Conn. • Waterville, Maine • London

Christine Nasso, *Publisher*
Elizabeth Des Chenes, *Managing Editor*

© 2007 Thomson Gale, a part of The Thomson Corporation.

Thomson and Star logo are trademarks and Gale and Greenhaven Press are registered trademarks used herein under license.

For more information, contact:
Greenhaven Press
27500 Drake Rd.
Farmington Hills, MI 48331-3535
Or you can visit our Internet site at http://www.gale.com

LIBRARY OF CONGRESS CATALOGING-IN-PUBLICATION DATA

Will the world run out of fresh water? / Debra A. Miller, book editor.
   p. cm. -- (At issue)
Includes bibliographical references and index.
ISBN-13: 978-0-7377-3403-4 (hardcover)
ISBN-13: 978-0-7377-3404-1 (pbk.)
  1. Water-supply--Juvenile literature. 2. Water consumption--Juvenile literature.
I. Miller, Debra A.
  TD348.W54 2007
  363.6'1--dc22

                     2006039097

ISBN-10: 0-7377-3403-5 (hardcover)
ISBN-10: 0-7377-3404-3 (pbk.)

Printed in the United States of America
10 9 8 7 6 5 4 3 2 1

Contents

Introduction   7

1. Billions of People Will Run Out of Fresh   11
   Water by 2050
   Gayle Ehrenman

2. One-Third of the World Is Already Facing   20
   Water Scarcity
   Consultative Group on International
   Agricultural Research

3. The Water Crisis Also Affects   25
   Rich Countries
   Phil Dickie

4. Global Warming Will Exacerbate   35
   Water Problems
   Environment News Service

5. The Scarcity of Water Could Lead to War   42
   Roman Kupchinsky

6. The Water Crisis Does Not Have to   47
   Lead to War
   Aaron T. Wolf, Annika Kramer, Alexander
   Carius, and Geoffrey D. Dabelko

7. The Risks of Privatization Must Be Balanced   54
   by Government Oversight
   Peter H. Gleick, Gary Wolff, Elizabeth L.
   Chalecki, and Rachel Reyes

8. Privatization Has Failed to Address the Water   73
   Problem in Developing Nations
   John Vidal

9. Technological Solutions Alone May Not   77
   Solve the Water Crisis
   Sam Jaffe

10. Better Water Management Is the Key to   87
    Solving the Water Crisis
    David B. Brooks

11. Supply and Demand Strategies Must Be   97
    Applied to Alleviate Water Problems
    Center for Strategic and International Studies

12. Worldwide Efforts Are Necessary to Prevent   103
    a World Water Crisis
    *UN/WWAP (United Nations/World Water
    Assessment Programme)*

Organizations to Contact   111

Bibliography   115

Index   122

Introduction

The earth's precious fresh water resources are stretched very thinly, and according to most scholars, the world faces an impending water crisis. Experts point to industrialization, massive population growth, and an accompanying expansion of agriculture in the last century as depleting some of these water sources, and note that others have been contaminated by pollution from fertilizers and pesticides. Global warming is also cited as adding to water scarcity problems. Already, many nations, even developed countries, are beginning to face water challenges, and these challenges are projected to increase as populations grow. In some parts of the world, however, people will likely face extremely dire water shortages and the competition for water could become fierce, possibly even leading to military conflicts. This is especially true for regions such as the Middle East, which already face difficult political tensions. Indeed, many commentators predict that water, rather than oil, will soon become the most precious liquid in the Middle East.

Arab-Israeli Water Disputes

Experts say the Middle East has already witnessed one war over water. The 1967 Six-Day War between Israel and the Arab countries of Egypt, Syria, and Jordan was caused, in part, because of conflicts over the waters of the Jordan River, a water resource shared by Israel, Jordan, Syria, Lebanon, and the Palestinians. In 1964 Israel completed the National Water Carrier project, a system of canals and pipes to bring water from the Jordan River to the deserts in southern Israel. Arab states opposed the Israeli water project and responded by beginning construction of the Headwater Diversion Plan, a project designed to divert the headwaters of the Jordan River into a dam to serve Jordan and Syria, and into the Litani River in Lebanon. The Arab plan would have reduced Israel's water by about 35 percent.

The Arab diversion project was never completed, however, because Israel attacked the construction site in Syria in 1965. The Israeli attacks initiated a long series of border attacks and incidents between Syria and Israel that ultimately escalated to all-out war in 1967. During the 1967 war, Israel occupied the Golan Heights, a territory belonging to Syria, and the West Bank, a territory once part of Jordan. This gave Israel control over large parts of the Jordan River, including its headwaters and parts of its main tributary (the Yarmuk River), as well as aquifers, or underground reservoirs, located in the occupied territories.

Today, water competition continues to be part of the on-going Arab-Israeli conflict. After the 1967 war, Israel increased its water usage from the Jordan River and also began tapping regional aquifers. Over the years, Israeli population growth increased its domestic and agricultural water usage even more. Israel's water gains, however, were a loss for surrounding Arab states and the Palestinians living in the occupied territories, contributing to rising Arab-Israeli tensions. A 1994 treaty between Jordan and Israel established water-sharing guidelines for water from the Jordan and Yarmuk Rivers, but Israel halved its annual water allocation to Jordan in 1999, and today Jordan is facing an escalating water deficit that is expected to reach crisis proportions by 2010. Israel is also at odds with the Palestinians over access to the West Bank Mountain Aquifer, the source of about one-third of Israel's water supply and about 80 percent of Palestinian fresh water. According to human rights advocates, Israelis use about 350 liters of water a day, but many Palestinians live on less than 100 liters each day, the minimum recommended by the World Health Organization. Many observers speculate that these water disputes are one of the main obstacles to resolution of the Arab-Israeli conflict.

Other Middle East Water Disputes

The Arab-Israeli crisis is not the only Middle East hotspot involving water, however. The countries of Turkey, Syria, and Iraq are embroiled in a dispute over water from the Euphrates, a river that originates in Turkey and flows through Syria and Iraq. Turkey and Syria signed an agreement in 1987 ensuring Syria access to Euphrates water, but to supply its growing population with electricity and food, Turkey is building the Southeast Anatolia Project (GAP), a plan to create twenty-two dams that will give Turkey total control over the river's headwaters. In 1990 Turkey demonstrated its new control by withdrawing water to fill a recently built dam; this action caused a 75 percent drop in downstream water for a full month. Once GAP is fully operational, it could reduce Euphrates water to Syria by 40 percent and to Iraq by up to 80 percent—worrisome projections that threaten to produce dangerous future conflicts.

Another crisis point has emerged concerning the Nile River, a river that originates in Ethiopia and flows through Egypt and Sudan, providing both downstream countries with most of their fresh water. Egypt and Sudan entered an agreement in 1959 to share the river's waters, but rapid population growth in both countries has increased dependence on Nile resources. At the same time, Ethiopia has begun to develop its agriculture industry and is making new claims on the Nile's headwaters—a stance that could threaten both Egypt and Sudan. All of these developments have led to increasing tensions in the northern Africa region in the Middle East.

Meanwhile, Saudi Arabia, which lacks access to rivers or other bodies of fresh water, is rapidly withdrawing water from the Persian Gulf region's underground water reservoirs, mostly for agricultural purposes. This course of action threatens to completely deplete this important, finite water source in just twenty to thirty years. This situation, and the Saudi-government's search for new water aquifers, has caused tensions between Saudi Arabia and many of its neighbors on the Persian Gulf peninsula.

The water problems in the Middle East are just one aspect of the overall world water crisis, however. The authors in *At Issue: Will the World Run Out of Fresh Water?* examine the issue of the water crisis, its effects, and its possible solutions from a variety of perspectives. Some commentators say preventing water shortages will depend on technological solutions, while others advocate for better conservation, changes in the way water is managed and used, or new agreements to equitably distribute the world's water resources. Solving the water crisis will surely be difficult, but it may be possible—if only because water is so important to life itself.

1

Billions of People Will Run Out of Fresh Water by 2050

Gayle Ehrenman

About the Author*: Gayle Ehrenman is an associate editor at* Mechanical Engineering, *a weekly magazine that focuses on mechanical engineering's leading role in technological developments.*

Although much of the Earth's surface is covered with water, the world is on the verge of a global water crisis. Today, only parts of the world suffer from a lack of clean, fresh water, but this crisis will ultimately affect all countries and threaten their ability to maintain health and provide adequate food supplies. Indeed, only a tiny part of Earth's water is fresh water suitable for drinking and it is not equitably distributed. Asia, for example, has only 36 percent of the world's water resource but is home to 60 percent of the world's population. Fresh water supplies are also reduced by pollution and wastes. Already, a large number of people lack safe drinking water—a problem that causes high rates of infection from water-related diseases in many developing countries. The nature of the crisis varies depending on whether a region is rural or urban, developing or industrial. In developing countries, growing water demands by dense urban populations and a lack of infrastructure and sanitation are the main problems, while in wealthy nations the primary concern may be water quality and contamination. Overuse of water by agriculture and drought are also major factors. Although there are some

Gayle Ehrenman, "Not a Drop to Drink: By the Middle of This Century, 7 Billion People Could Be Short of Water. At Best, It Will bBe 2 Billion People," *Mechanical Engineering-CIME*, vol. 125, September 2003, p. 9. Copyright 2003 American Society of Mechanical Engineers. Reproduced by permission.

promising technologies and strategies, averting a water crisis will be a massive challenge for all nations.

Approximately 71 percent of the Earth's surface is covered with water. Yet, by all accounts, the world is on the verge of a water crisis. What exactly that water crisis entails, or when it will hit, depends on what part of the world you're looking at. In drought-plagued regions, such as Zimbabwe, Mauritania, and the western United States, the water crisis has already begun. "At this point in time, the water crisis isn't global, but there are pockets of crisis," said Hugh Turral, a theme leader and principal researcher for the International Water Management Institute in Colombo, Sri Lanka. "Right now, in most parts of the world, the crisis is one of governance. Long-term, there will be problems with scarcity around the world."

In its first World Water Development Report, Water for People, Water for Life, the United Nations concurred, stating: "Attitude and behavior problems lie at the heart of the crisis. Inertia at leadership level and a world population not fully aware of the scale of the problem means we fail to take the needed timely corrective actions." The World Water Development Report was produced by the World Water Assessment Programme, whose secretariat is hosted by UNESCO [United Nations Educational, Scientific and Cultural Organization]. "Of all the social and natural crises we humans face, the water crisis is the one that lies at the heart of our survival and that of our planet Earth," said UNESCO's director-general, Koichiro Matsuura, in a prepared statement. "No region will be spared from the impact of this crisis, which touches every facet of life, from the health of children to the ability of nations to secure food for their citizens."

Freshwater—A Limited Resource

Though water is indeed a renewable resource, to a certain extent it is also a finite one. Only 2.53 percent of the Earth's water is fresh, and some two-thirds of that is locked up in glaciers and permanent snow cover. Regionally, the distribution of that water is far from equitable. Asia is particularly hard hit, with just 36 percent of the world's water resources supporting 60 percent of the world's population, according to the U.N.'s World Water Report. Africa, though it has just 11 percent of the world's available fresh water, has a better balance since it has 13 percent of the world's population.

A large percentage of the world's population lacks access to safe drinking water. . . . The end result is a staggering rate of infection from water-related diseases.

Freshwater resources are reduced by pollution. The U.N. report estimates that some 2 million tons of waste per day are disposed of within waters. This waste includes industrial trash and chemicals, human waste, and agricultural runoff, such as fertilizers, pesticides, and pesticide residue. The World Water Report estimates that global wastewater production is roughly 1,500 cubic kilometers [1.21 million acre feet] per year. Assuming that 1 liter [1.06 quarts] of wastewater pollutes about 8 liters [8.45 quarts] of freshwater, the present burden of water pollution may be as high as 12,000 km³ [9.7 billion acre feet]. The U.N. estimates that 50 percent of the population of developing countries depends on polluted water sources.

Factoring in the availability of fresh water, current rates of pollution, and the potential for climate change—including a trend toward more frequent extreme weather conditions, such as floods and droughts—the World Water Report predicts that by the middle of this century, at worst, 7 billion people in 60 countries will be short of water; at best, 2 billion people in 48 countries will suffer shortages.

While water shortages are not widespread at the present time, a large percentage of the world's population lacks access to safe drinking water. Currently, 1.1 billion people lack access to an "improved" water supply (defined as water that has been at least marginally treated to remove chemical or biological contaminants). Some 2.4 billion people lack access to adequate sanitation. The end result is a staggering rate of infection from water-related diseases, particularly among the poor in developing countries. In 2000, roughly 2.2 million people died from water sanitation–associated diseases. An estimated 1 million more died from malaria, according to the World Water Report. If improved water supply and basic sanitation were extended to the currently unserved population, mortality from such water and hygiene-related diseases would be reduced by 17 percent annually. If a piped, well-regulated water supply and full sanitation were provided, the rate of disease would drop 70 percent annually, the report predicted.

Where the Water Goes

What exactly constitutes a water crisis varies greatly, according to type of environment: rural or urban community, developing or industrial nation. In rural areas, the conflict is one of agricultural overuse, groundwater contamination, and, in some parts of the world, lack of infrastructure and sanitation. In urban areas, the crisis is primarily one of insufficient water to support the dense population. In developing nations, the primary concern is simply providing water to people, while water quality may take a backseat. In industrial nations, where the infrastructure for providing drinking water to the majority of the population is already in place, the concern turns to maintaining the level of service and the quality of the water supply.

Irrigation accounts for 70 percent of all water usage. Industry accounts for another 22 percent of the total water use, and the remaining 8 percent falls to domestic use.

"In developing countries, the problem is in feeding a growing population," said Turral of the Water Management Institute. The population in developing countries is increasing at roughly 2 to 2.5 percent a year, which puts a significant strain on agriculture. "Long-term, there's going to be a need to increase food production by 40 percent in developing nations, without expanding the irrigated area," he said. This will necessitate improvements in the productivity of land and water. Developing countries will have to increase crop yield, and improve water management and usage. "There's a tremendous impetus to keep on using irrigation to offset poverty in developing countries," he said.

According to the World Water Report, irrigation accounts for 70 percent of all water usage. Industry accounts for another 22 percent of total water use, and the remaining 8 percent falls to domestic use. Those percentages are expected to change, as the population shifts in most parts of the world from rural areas to urban. Currently, the World Water Report estimates that about 48 percent of the world's population lives in towns and cities. By 2030, that number is expected to rise to 60 percent. Cities are generally more efficient users of water than agriculture, Turral said. "Cities don't consume water" he said. "They typically use water and return it." But this causes its own set of problems.

Different Countries, Different Concerns

Pakistan, Bangladesh, and China are heavy users of groundwater, according to Turral, and that practice has its own problems of contamination and pollution. "When you overdraw groundwater, it degrades the quality of that water, and you see the effects down the line," he said. For example, in Bangladesh, a high level of naturally occurring arsenic, coupled with overdrafting of the groundwater supply, has created a serious problem that the public water system is not equipped to deal with. According to Sandra Postel, director of the Global Water Policy Project in Amherst, Massachusetts, and a senior fellow at the Worldwatch Institute, overpumping is widespread in China's north-central plain, which produces some 40 percent of the nation's grain. Across a wide area, water tables have been dropping 1 to 1.5 meters a year, even as the nation's water demands continue to climb.

In Africa, there is sufficient groundwater of high enough quality to support a larger population. However, the infrastructure is lacking to bring the water to the people, according to the Water Management Institute's Turral. High fuel costs and inefficient pumping systems are major factors contributing to the water crisis in this part of the world.

In the western United States, the problems are largely the result of insufficient water to serve a rapidly growing population, according to Ane Deister, chair of the American Water Works Association's conservation division, and general manager of the El Dorado Irrigation District, in Placerville, Calif. "Drought is our biggest problem in California," Deister said. "It's both an urban and agricultural problem that we need to prepare for better. At the federal level, there's a strong recognition that the impact of drought on agriculture is economically devastating." According to the National Drought Mitigation Center's U.S. Drought Monitor, moderate to severe drought conditions have been ongoing in the West, Southwest, and Pacific Northwest. There is no end in sight to these problems, according to forecasts. "Understanding the science of drought and preparing for it is crucial to our country's well-being," said Deister. "We need a better monitoring and prediction network so weather forecasters can communicate; we need more studies of crops that are drought resistant long-term; we need preparedness plans; and we need to educate and inform the public, who will be impacted by this crisis."

Compounding the drought problems is a reduction in the amount of surplus Colorado River water available to surrounding states. This water has been a bone of contention for California, Nevada, Arizona, Colorado, New Mexico, Utah, and Wyoming. California has been ordered by the U.S. Department of the Interior to gradually reduce its draw of the

Colorado River from 5.2 million acre-feet to 4.4 million. At press time, a proposed transfer of water from the farming communities of the Imperial Valley to the densely populated and underserved city of San Diego to offset the loss of the Colorado River water had not been completed.

There are no easy solutions to the world's water crises, but there are some promising technologies.

Further complicating matters, many areas of California and the rest of the United States are plagued by ground water that is contaminated with methyl-tertiary-butyl ether [MTBE] and perchlorate, both of which are potentially hazardous to humans. No federal standards yet exist for acceptable levels of either contaminant. MTBE is a fuel oxygenate that leaches into the groundwater from faulty underground storage tanks. Santa Monica, Calif., has been identified as suffering from some of the worst MTBE contamination, according to Deister. Perchlorate can be naturally occurring or man-made. Perch is used in solid rocket propellant, as well as in nuclear reactors and electronic tubes. Both Santa Ana and Santa Clara, Calif., have identified serious perchlorate contamination, Deister said.

Possible Solutions

There are no easy solutions to the world's water crises, but there are some promising technologies. Desalination, in particular, has been identified as a promising technology for creating new sources of potable water. "Desalination is an area of major interest in Southern California coastal areas, which are currently very Colorado River water dependent," Deister said. "The technology has become so much more affordable that it's a viable solution for coastal areas that need a new source of water." Five large municipal water agencies, all based in California, have joined together to form the United States De-

salination Coalition. Its goal is to ask Congress to approve leg-
islation aimed at providing financial incentives and grants for
the development of desalination treatment facilities. Desalination is also gaining traction in Florida, where North America's
largest seawater desalination plant is under construction for
Tampa Bay Water. The Brazos River Authority in Waco, Texas,
also expect to begin work on a seawater desalination facility
soon.

Aquifer storage and recovery offers another alternative for
drought-plagued communities. The method uses aquifer for-
mations to collect water when it is plentiful and to store it in
an environmentally friendly way. It doesn't create a new supply of water, but rather stores available water efficiently. The
Metropolitan Water District of Southern California has undertaken some major projects in this arena. . . .

Water recycling and reuse are perhaps the cornerstone
techniques for helping to drought-proof communities, according to Deister. "Recycling provides a safe and reliable source of
water, and a good way to keep wastewater from entering the
environment," she said. Deister's own El Dorado Irrigation
District, which lies midway between Sacramento and South
Lake Tahoe, currently uses recycled wastewater to irrigate golf
courses and public grass plots. The district also recently received approval to use the water in residential gardens.

While recycled wastewater in the United States is carefully
treated and used only for non-consumable and non-hygiene-
related purposes, this isn't always the case in developing countries. According to Turral in Sri Lanka, many cities of Asia and
Africa are reusing wastewater for irrigation, but they're not
necessarily treating it. This exposes irrigation workers and
even consumers to parasites, as well as to organic, chemical,
and heavy metal contaminants, according to the World Water
Report.

A better alternative in agricultural developing countries is
improving irrigation technology to use less water. Remote

sensing, sprinkler irrigation, hydrodynamic gates on irrigation canals, and micro-irrigation kits for small farms could all go a long way to improve the efficiency of irrigation, Turral said. Automatic controls for canal gates are already in place in Morocco, Iran, Iraq, and Pakistan. But there is still potential for improvement.

Averting a water crisis is a massive undertaking that will require a combination [of] conservation, new technology, and cooperation among competing interests. Contaminated water will have to be cleaned up, while further pollution is reduced. And, new sources of water will need to be found if the constantly growing demand for suitable water for drinking, farming, and industry is to be met.

2

One-Third of the World Is Already Facing Water Scarcity

Consultative Group on International Agricultural Research

About the Author: *The Consultative Group on International Agricultural Research is an agricultural research organization dedicated to stimulating agricultural growth, raising farmers' incomes, and protecting the environment.*

Earlier findings had predicted that one-third of the world would be affected by water shortages by 2025, but a 2006 study called the Comprehensive Assessment of Water Management in Agriculture indicated that one of every three people is already facing problems of water scarcity. The study, carried out by seven-hundred experts from around the world over the last five years, found that the people most affected live in river basins and other areas where the water is either overused or cannot be accessed due to the lack of infrastructure. Access to safe and affordable water is necessary to allow the world's poor to escape poverty, but the choice is either to continue to damage the environment or make better use of the water people already use. Africa, one of the poorest areas, has great potential for increasing agricultural yields without using more water. Other regions facing water scarcity are Egypt, Australia, and the Aral Sea in Uzbekistan and Kazakhstan. The water crisis is threatening, but there are bright spots. There are low-cost technologies that can be employed to access water; waste-water can be recycled; and better irrigation methods can help reduce water waste. Solving the wa-

Consultative Group on International Agricultural Research, "One Third of the Population Faces Water Scarcity Today," www.iwmi.cgiar.org/Press/releases/CA%20Launch%20Press%20Release_Final.pdf, August 21, 2006. Reproduced by permission.

ter problem will also require making tough choices about how to allocate and manage water; otherwise, the environment will continue to be destroyed.

One in three people is enduring one form or another of water scarcity, according to new findings released by the Comprehensive Assessment of Water Management in Agriculture at World Water Week in Stockholm [August 20–26, 2006]. These alarming findings totally overrun predictions that this situation would come to pass in 2025. "Worrisome predictions in 2000 had forecast that one third of the world population would be affected by water scarcity by 2025. Our findings from the just-concluded research show the situation to be even worse," says Frank Rijsberman, Director General of the International Water Management Institute (IWMI). "Already in 2005, more than a third of the world population is affected by water scarcity. We will have to change business as usual in order to deal with growing scarcity water crisis we see in some countries like India, China, and the Colorado River basin of USA and Mexico."

The Comprehensive Assessment Study

The Comprehensive Assessment, carried out by 700 experts from around the world over the last five years, indicates that one third of the world's population is currently living in places where water is either over-used—leading to falling groundwater levels and drying rivers—or can not be accessed due to the absence of the appropriate infrastructure.

The Assessment, the first of its kind critically examining policies and practices of water use and development in the agricultural sector over the last 50 years, was co-sponsored by the CGIAR [Consultative Group on International Agricultural Research], FAO [Food and Agriculture Organization of the United Nations], the Ramsar Convention on Wetlands, and the Convention on Biological Diversity in a bid to find solutions to the challenge of balancing the water-food-environment

21

needs. It was spearheaded by IWMI, one of 15 agricultural research centres supported by the CGIAR that are striving to increase food production, increase rural incomes, and safeguard the environment.

Rijsberman explained: "Our results show that one quarter of the world's population live in river basins where water is physically scarce—water is over-used and people are affected by environmental consequences from falling groundwater levels to dying rivers that no longer reach the sea. Another one billion people live in river basins where water is economically scarce—water is available in rivers and aquifers, but the infrastructure is lacking to make this water available to people."

Water and Poverty

Access to reliable, safe and affordable water is understood and accepted as a key step out of poverty for the world's 800 million rural poor. Many more people dependent on rivers, lakes and other wetlands risk falling into poverty because of declining groundwater supplies, loss of water rights and access, pollution, flooding and drought.

David Molden who led the Comprehensive Assessment says, "To feed the growing population and reduce malnourishment, the world has three choices: expand irrigation by diverting more water to agriculture and building more dams, at a major cost to the environment; expand the area under rain-fed agriculture at the expense of natural areas through massive deforestation and other habitat destruction; or do more with the water we already use. We must grow more crop per drop, more meat and milk per drop, and more fish per drop."

Africa's savannahs—which have most of the world's poorest people who typically rely on rain-fed agriculture—are singled out by the Assessment as holding the greatest potential for increasing water productivity, increasing agricultural yields per unit water used.

"The savannahs are fragile and the rainfall is variable; making them productive systems for farmers is very difficult," says Rijsberman. "But this year, the World Food Prize goes to three scientists who have done exactly that for the Brazilian savannahs, the cerrados. The Brazilians used improved varieties of African grasses to conquer their savannahs. They proved that it can be done. The same miracle needs to be repeated in Africa."

Agriculture uses up to 70 times more water to produce food than is used in drinking and other domestic purposes, including cooking, washing and bathing.

Areas of Water Scarcity

Already the consequences of water scarcity are evident in a number of countries. Egypt imports more than half of its food because it does not have enough water to grow it domestically. Australia is faced with major water scarcity in the Murray-Darling Basin as a result of diverting large quantities of water for use in agriculture. The Aral Sea disaster [in Uzbekistan and Kazakhstan] is another example where massive diversions of water to agriculture have caused widespread water scarcity, and one of the world's worst environmental disasters.

Agriculture uses up to 70 times more water to produce food than is used in drinking and other domestic purposes, including cooking, washing and bathing. As a rule of thumb, each calorie consumed as food requires about one litre [1.06 quarts] of water to produce. In Thailand, the daily water required to grow food is about 2800 litres per person per day—40 percent for cereals, 20 percent for animal products and the rest for pulses, fruits, sugar and oils. Italians use 3300 litres per person per day, half for ham and cheese and a third for pasta and bread. Clearly livestock and fish will play a significant role in future water use, but remarkably their importance is underestimated in water resources management.

Bright Spots

Despite the impending threat, the Assessment identifies numerous bright spots—innovative approaches that hold potential for the future. These include very low cost technologies that facilitate access to, and use of water by, the rural poor. With health issues addressed, for example, people can effectively use urban wastewaters as a productive resource. Irrigation could also be reformed and transformed to reduce water wastage and increase productivity.

There will be many difficult choices entailing tradeoffs between city and agriculture users, between food production and the environment, and between fishers and farmers. There is simply not enough water to go around for all needs, yet allocation choices have to be made. In closed basins, where all water has already been allocated, giving water to one group means taking water away from another.

"The Assessment shows that while a third of the world population faces water scarcity, it is not because there is not enough water to go round, but because of choices people make," Molden says. "It is possible to reduce water scarcity, feed people and address poverty, but the key trade-off is with the environment. People and their governments will face some tough decisions on how to allocate and manage water. Not all situations are going to be a win-win for the parties involved, and in most cases there are winners and losers. If you don't consciously debate and make tough choices, more people, especially the poor, and the environment will continue to pay the price."

3

The Water Crisis Also Affects Rich Countries

Phil Dickie

About the Author*: Phil Dickie is an award-winning investigative journalist from Queensland, Australia, who is known for his environmental writing. He currently is editor of the* Brisbane Line, *a newsletter published by the Brisbane Institute, an independent public policy organization in Australia that seeks to promote exchanges of ideas through seminars, policy briefings, and conferences.*

The world water crisis affects both rich and poor nations. There is only a very limited amount of usable freshwater on the earth and the amount of freshwater available to each person is decreasing due to population growth, climate change, and water loss caused by contaminants and pollutants. Some of the developed regions most affected are Europe, the United States, Australia, and Japan. Some of the common problems faced by developed nations include: exhaustion of water supplies due to large-scale industrial usage and growing populations; political conflict over water use and environmental issues; serious contamination of water from salt and agricultural pollutants; human actions that have changed natural water flows; and improper pricing of water used in agriculture. The developed world generally accepts that water must be used more efficiently and made available again to the environment to allow natural water systems to function, but this effort faces enormous political obstacles. The

Phil Dickie, "Rich Countries, Poor Water," *WWF Freshwater Fund*, 2006. © 2006 WWF—the environmental conservation organisation. Some rights reserved. Reproduced by permission.

main challenges ahead will include: properly valuing water; striking a balance between conservation and consumption so that water is left over for the environment; allowing some natural flooding to occur; repairing aging water infrastructures; raising prices for agricultural water; reducing pollution and contamination; and learning more about natural water cycles and processes. In addition, the developed world, as a disproportionate user of freshwater, must also take actions to more fairly and sustainably use the world's water resources.

The most recent global analysis of human access to the fresh water that underpins all societies shows a steadily worsening situation. According to the 2006 UN World Water development Report, 1.1 billion people around the world lack access to improved water supplies and 2.6 billion lack access to improved sanitation and "In many parts of the world, available water quantity is decreasing and quality is worsening". Most of these people live in the world's poorest countries, but as this report shows, there are major and mounting challenges on water facing the wealthier nations as well. The report is aptly titled "Water—A Shared Responsibility", a reflection of a rapidly growing realisation that the availability of adequate water is among the most basic and most urgent of the common issues faced by rich and poor nations alike.

Limited Freshwater

Excluding the water of the seas and the icecaps, an astoundingly small proportion of the water essential to all terrestrial life is actually available. Per person, that small proportion of useable freshwater is also set to decrease as a consequence of population growth, climate change and substantial water supply losses through the contamination of water sources. This ethnocentric view is the cause of increasing alarm that sometimes neglects the fact that water is being lost to all life. Indeed, there is growing awareness that the last half century of human interventions with water flows have significantly altered global hydrology. Just as with the excess production of greenhouse gases, this may have consequences that are themselves threatening the conditions for life.

Terms such as "world water crisis" are not new, but they are overwhelmingly applied to the unmet water needs and the looming water catastrophes of the developing world. This survey finds that the world's wealthier nations also face a water crisis, as the profligate water use and abuse of the past and new requirements for "environmental water" confront and in some cases outrun available supplies.

Region in Crisis

In Europe, countries fronting the Atlantic Ocean are suffering recurring droughts, while water intensive tourism and an explosion of irrigated agriculture are endangering the water resources of the Mediterranean. It is now apparent that intensive pollution remediation in Europe's heartland will not be able to salvage some contaminated water sources—while the much worse contamination issues of Eastern Europe are yet to be substantially addressed. The European Union Water Framework Directive is a much needed initiative to systematically tackle Europe's water issues by 2015, but implementation is patchy in some countries.

In the USA, large areas are already using substantially more water than can be naturally replenished. This situation will only be further exacerbated by climate change scenarios of lower rainfall, increased evaporation and changed snowmelt patterns. Salinity threatens important irrigation areas and there is increasing anxiety over the level of contamination with chemicals and pathogens in water sources and water supplies. The main mechanisms for controlling pollution are themselves under threat

In Australia, the driest continent is well on its way to becoming drier. Nearly all of Australia's major cities have applied water restrictions and efficiency measures while they grapple with current and projected shortages in supply. Salinity is a major threat to a large proportion of Australia's key agricultural areas and the drinking water supplies of the nation's fifth largest city. Saving the country's largest river system has become a flagship programme with some restoration of environmental flows announced but much more needed.

From Seville to Sacramento to Sydney, water is now a key ... political issue at the local, regional and national level.

Japan has high rainfall, but high population can mean surprisingly low levels of water per capita. Japanese cities can suffer both shortages of water and damaging floods. Contamination of water supplies, including groundwater aquifers, is an extremely serious issue in many areas. However, there is also a serious commitment to better management of Japan's water resources, which extends to repairing and better protecting damaged natural areas and to exporting expertise in better water management and protection.

Common Problems

Exhaustion of water supplies Supporting large scale industry and growing populations using water at high rates has come close to exhausting the water supplies of some first world cities and is a looming threat for many if not most others. Most long established cities have already exploited their naturally or politically feasible options for reservoir capacity and many are seeing levels dropping in the groundwater supplies they have become heavily and in some cases exclusively dependent on. Among the options being considered and in some cases implemented are rainfall capture, water recycling and "sewer mining", water transport from ever more remote locations, buying in of water and desalinating seawater.

Water-related conflict From Seville [Spain] to Sacramento [California] to Sydney [Australia], water is now a key—sometimes the key—political issue at the local, regional and national level. Significant water related conflicts commonly arise over infrastructure proposals, between catchments, between rural and urban water users, and between irrigators and virtually all other water users. Much of the conflict is over environmental issues such as the protection of catchments, maintaining flow in rivers and responsibility for pollution.

Water contamination Although there have been improvements in many areas, many first world waters still suffer from serious and long lasting contamination. The main contaminant is salt, a particular problem for many irrigated areas and coastal areas with over-exploited aquifers. The next most commonly detected contaminants by far are fertilizer and pesticide residues from agriculture which in some areas have percolated down to deep aquifers. But the full list of potential contaminants is long and incomplete, and contains numerous chemicals never tested for their toxicity, human pathogens, and toxic soil components such as arsenic mobilised by poor water management processes. New reasons for anxiety emerge regularly—the USA's worst water poisoning incident was caused by a pathogen identified less than 20 years earlier and a wide class of chemicals known as "endocrine disruptors" are under suspicion for their suspected ability to disrupt body functioning. Investigations are beginning into the effects of minute but accumulating pharmaceutical, medicinal and veterinary wastes.

Degraded landscape functioning Catchments that have been cleared, rivers that don't flow, floodplains that have been developed and wetlands that have been drained are not performing their ecosystem functions within the landscapes of the developed world. More and more the consequences of this degraded functioning are needing to be addressed to reduce health and economic impacts, to protect key environmental or economic assets or to reduce the likelihood of catastrophic events.

It is now generally well accepted in the developed world that water must be used more efficiently and that water must be made available again to the environment.

Economic burdens Water is an essential economic commodity. Increases in the costs of sourcing, supplying and treating water to an acceptable standard have been steadily escalating, as have been the costs of treating and disposing of waste water. Moreover, the trend to more environmentally and economically appropriate pricing of water . . . still has some way to go. Still to come in most developed countries is the proper valuation of water used in agriculture, in most nations by far the largest user of freshwater. Such measures drive efficiency, but are also adding to the cost base of the economy. Many first world cities are losing massive amounts of water and risking community health and groundwater contamination through leaks from mains and sewers. Dealing with this issue, often the single most effective urban conservation measure, is both costly and a source of conflict between privately operated water providers and regulatory bodies.

Choices for the Future

At the rhetoric level, it is now generally well accepted in the developed world that water must be used more efficiently and that water must be made available again to the environment in sufficient quantity for natural systems to function and deliver what are sometimes called their "ecosystem services." Many countries also recognise that extensive—and very expensive—repairs are required to reduce some of the damage inflicted on water systems and catchments in the past. Putting the rhetoric into practice in the face of habitual practice and intense lobbying by vested interests has been very difficult.

What the developed world has, however, is choice. It can persist with business as usual under a veneer of rhetoric about conservation and face the consequences further down the track—harder to secure supplies of water, ever more expensive treatment, ever increasing impacts on the economy and ever larger exposure to catastrophic events. Or it can, as several countries have been doing, continue with the effort to match current water use with natural water realities and, as much as possible, build the resilience of human and natural water systems against challenges such as increased demands in the face of greater climate variability.

Challenges Ahead

Even in the best performing countries, conservation has a long way to go. The seven key challenges are to:

1. *Properly value water* and the natural features and services offered by catchments, streams, aquifers, floodplains and wetlands. Conserve the environment of watersheds as the source of water for people and nature. Establish an organisation to manage each river basin.

2. *Agree on the balance* between conservation and water consumption so that the quantity and timing of water abstractions leave sufficient "environmental flows" to maintain ecological health of rivers, lakes and other wetland habitats at acceptable levels.

3. *Change attitudes to water.* For instance, it is becoming accepted that the effort to prevent all flooding leads to more catastrophic floods and that it is not only safer but also beneficial to give rivers room and restore or mimic natural systems that accommodate periodic flooding.

4. *Modify or repair* aging or inappropriate infrastructure, to reduce wastage, contamination and disruption to natural processes

5. *Bring agriculture into line.* In general the largest by far water user, agriculture, faces lower prices for water and lower expectations that it will use water efficiently and manage its wastes. Agricultural chemicals are, after salt, the most common contaminants of water. As sewage treatment improves, intensive livestock farming and aquaculture become the largest source of pathogens in water.

6. *Reduce the contamination of water.* A staggering array of contaminants is finding its way into water supplies. Only a minority are tested for. A recent history of nasty surprises suggests that the effects of some of these substances are not yet known, and that some we do know are damaging will later be found to be more damaging than suspected at smaller concentrations than were previously thought acceptable.

7. *Build up our knowledge.* Understanding of natural water cycles and processes remains sketchy, particularly on elements of water systems that are not immediately visible or obvious such as vapour cycles and aquifers. We are continually reminded that all the elements of the system are interconnected and that the more uninformed our interventions are, the greater the likelihood of unexpected outcomes.

Obligations to the World

For the developed world, while local action is clearly needed, it is not sufficient to act locally. The world's water is not equally shared and there is deservedly a focus on the unmet water needs of the world's poor. Daily per capita use of water in residential areas is estimated at 350 litres in North America and Japan, 200 litres in Europe and 10-20 litres in sub-Saharan

Africa. In general, the first world has more of the world's freshwater resources and uses more of the world's freshwater resources—either directly or more indirectly as when the poor world's water is disproportionately used or contaminated in growing the cash crops or providing the minerals and energy consumed by the relatively wealthy.

Sometimes measured as "virtual water", the inflows of water embodied in imported products mean that the "water footprints" of developed nations can be out of all proportion to domestic water supplies. The UNESCO-IHE [United Nations Educational, Scientific and Cultural Organization International Hydrological Programme] Water Institute cites the examples of China with a water footprint of 700 cubic metres [.57 acre foot] per capita per year overwhelmingly sourced from within China and Japan, where 65 per cent of the 1150 cubic metres [.93 acre foot] per capita per year water footprint is sourced from outside Japan.

First world institutions have also played a role in some of the more damaging water infrastructure projects undertaken in the third world. While some water infrastructure projects have produced great benefits, in many the dislocations, disruptions to natural flow patterns that sustain food and fibre supplies and extensions to the range of disease carrying organisms have imposed great suffering on communities that enjoy few of the benefits. Processes to prevent such mistakes in the future, such as those set out by the World Commission on Dams, are still a long way from proper implementation.

Fairly and sustainably using the world's limited supplies of freshwater and ensuring that sufficient water is available to perform essential environmental functions are local, regional and global issues for all.

4

Global Warming Will Exacerbate Water Problems

Environment News Service

About the Author: *The Environment News Service (ENS) was established in 1990 and is the original international wire service for environmental news. Contributors and correspondents from around the world cover events and ENS news reports are frequently used by Reuters and other news services.*

The world water crisis is complicated by the effects of global warming. Nobel Prize winner in chemistry Mario Molina warned in March 2006 that if the current global warming trend continues, the temperatures of the planet will rise by eight degrees Celsius in this century. This climate change has caused intensifying rains and droughts, melting of the glaciers, and has exacerbated flooding and water scarcity. The year 2005 was the warmest in the last thousand years. Although modern responses to the water crisis have emphasized technology, United Nations officials stress the need to understand the relationship between water and cultural traditions and values in order to find sustainable water solutions. The global water crisis today is causing death, disease, and disasters around the world. Asia has experienced the most deaths from water disasters, but North America also has been affected, as shown by Hurricane Katrina. Africa, meanwhile, needs major water investment to develop a sustainable water policy and help alleviate widespread poverty and disease. Indeed, new investments in water management and development are essential for all developing countries. According to the World Bank, these investments must come from both public and private sources, but the privatization of water causes great fear among poor people who worry that they will not be able to afford the precious liquid.

An international meeting on the future of the world's fresh water resources [marked] World Water Day today [March 22, 2006] with a renewed effort to ensure that more clean drinking water reaches the 1.1 billion people who do not have access to safe water, but the crisis is complicated by the impacts of a warming climate, a world renowned atmospheric chemist told delegates. In addition to drinking water scarcity, about 2.6 billion people, four out of every 10, lack access to sanitation. This situation is a humanitarian crisis—dealing with it must move to the top of the global agenda, [said] ministers and water experts meeting . . . for the 4th World Water Forum.

The Global Warming Risk

In his keynote speech to the Forum . . . , Nobel Prize Winner in chemistry Mario Molina warned that climate change and inappropriate water management might intensify global warming by the end of this century, creating "an intolerable risk." If the current global warming trend is maintained, the temperature of the planet will rise eight degrees Celsius [14.4 degrees Fahrenheit] during this century, "an increase of historic proportions," said Molina, who shared the 1995 Nobel Prize in Chemistry for his work on the destruction of the ozone layer by chlorofluorocarbons.

Molina said intensifying rains and droughts are related to climate change and to the melting of glaciers. Climate change has exacerbated flooding and water scarcity, he said. The year 2005 "was the warmest in the last thousand years," Molina pointed out, showing charts of "paleo-climate data," extracted

from drops of water encapsulated within glaciers and information from the outer rings of trees in ancient forests.

Water and Culture

Director-General of UNESCO [United Nations Educational,
Scientific and Cultural Organization] Koïchiro Matsuura says
the theme of Water and Culture is of particular significance
for UNESCO, which is leading the activities surrounding this
year's World Water Day. "To achieve sustainable solutions that
contribute to equity, peace and development, water management and governance need to take proper account of cultural
and biological diversity," Matsuura said. "For this reason,
UNESCO believes that the cultural dimension of water de-
serves further exploration so that its many ramifications may
become better understood."

---

*The water crisis threatens the security, stability and sus-
tainability of the planet and consequently, humanity itself.*

Modern approaches to water resource management have
tended to be overwhelmingly technology-driven in their at-
tempt to solve the world's urgent water problems, he said.
Water-related extreme events, such as floods and droughts, kill
more people than any other natural disaster, and water-borne
diseases continue to cause the death of thousands of children
every day. Because of its growth and development, the human
population increasingly alters the quality and distribution of
water. "But the amount of fresh water on Earth, to be shared
among all forms of life, remains the same," said Matsuura.
"This situation imposes on humankind a responsibility to develop ethically sound systems of water governance." But, he
said, technology alone will not lead us to viable solutions.

"Traditional knowledge alerts us to the fact that water is
not merely a commodity," Matsuura said. "Since the dawn of

humanity, water has inspired us, giving life spiritually, materially, intellectually and emotionally. Sharing and applying the rich contents of our knowledge systems, including those of traditional and indigenous societies, as well as lessons learned from our historical interactions with water, may greatly contribute to finding solutions for today's water challenges."

"The nexus between culture and nature is the avenue for understanding resilience, creativity and adaptability in both social and ecological systems. In this perspective, sustainable water use and, hence, a sustainable future depend on the harmonious relationship between water and culture," the UNESCO director-general said. "Consequently," he said, "it is vital that water management and governance take cultural traditions, indigenous practices and societal values into serious account."

Death, Disease, and Disasters

The global water crisis is growing, UNESCO said in a statement to mark World Water Day. The water crisis threatens the security, stability and sustainability of the planet and consequently, humanity itself. This is why the period from 2005 to 2015 has been declared the International Decade for Action Water for Life.

Reiterating that lack of access to water is a major source of death and disease in the world, World Water Council President Loïc Fauchon announced the launch of the Council's Water for Schools initiative, which seeks to provide access to water in 1,000 schools in 10 countries.

During the Forum's plenary session on Tuesday, the director of the National Water Commission for Mexico Cristóbal Jaime announced an agreement by which an office of the World Meteorological Organization will be established in Mexico. Jaime reiterated an "urgent call" to the UN Secretary General's Advisory Board on Water and Sanitation to reduce by half the average number of deaths associated to water related disasters that will take place between now and the year 2015, as compared to the figures recorded for the decade from 1991-2000. Jaime said emergency aid funds should be established for preventive measures against disasters. "The international community might approve financing early warning systems and educational programs for the most vulnerable countries," he suggested.

Asia's Problems

The representatives of Asian countries Tuesday announced the creation of the Asia Pacific Water Forum in a region particularly hard hit by disasters. A recent UNESCAP [United Nations Economic and Social Commission for Asia and the Pacific] study showed that the Asian and Pacific region accounted for 91 per cent of the world's total deaths due to natural disaster. The average annual economic damage has increased from US$10.6 billion over the past five decades to US$29 billion over the past 15 years.

Ryutaro Hashimoto, former Prime Minister of Japan and president of the Japan Water Forum, and chair of the UN Advisory Board on Water and Sanitation, supported the agreement creating the Asia Pacific Water Forum. He reminded the audience that 60 percent of the world population lives in the Asia Pacific region and explored how to obtain financing for local water projects in his keynote address.

Kim Huk Su, executive secretary for the United Nations Economic and Social Commission for Asia and the Pacific (UNESCAP), said that there are two major priorities for the new regional forum—the need for tools to support Integrated Water Resource Management, and "radically" more effective risk management and risk prevention.

Asia and the Pacific is also the world's most disaster-prone region. A recent UNESCAP study showed that the region accounted for 91 percent of the world's total deaths due to natural disaster. The average annual economic damage has increased from US$10.6 billion over the past five decades to US$29 billion over the past 15 years.

Kim said that although the Asia-Pacific region has the highest economic growth rates in the world, it also has the lowest per-capita fresh water availability, and the highest number of people living below the poverty line.

Disasters in North America

North America has had its share of water disasters. At the plenary conference . . . on Risk Management, Carl Strock, chief of engineers of the U.S. Army Corps of Engineers (USACE), told delegates that a critical report on the performance of the government concerning Hurricane Katrina recognized that communication among different levels of government, logistics to deliver aid, and local warning systems did not perform as expected. "Disasters are now globalized phenomena," said Strock, "that require intervention from everyone."

Tropical storms in 2006 are expected to be even stronger than in 2005, the year hurricane Katrina and storm Stan wreaked havoc on the Mesoamerican region, said Max Campo, executive secretary of the Central American Regional Committee for Water Resources during a session of the IUCN-World Conservation Union at the Forum. Campos emphasized that, "We must integrate existing knowledge and technology in a systematic way so that citizens, with or without Internet access, can receive information on time so that people and their families can escape from catastrophic events."

Africa's Water Needs

The African continent has to date developed only 3.8 percent of its water resources for supply, irrigation and electrical power, according to the Regional Document on Africa, "Water Resources Development in Africa: Challenges Response and Prospective," prepared for discussion at the Forum. Africa's situation implies the need for hefty investment in various areas, and this investment must go hand in hand with changes in regional and national policy and capability, the document states.

Investment in water will spur progress in meeting the Millennium Development Goals. It will mitigate the scourge of malnutrition, food scarcity, poverty and disease that has led African nations to be counted among the poorest of the world, said the Regional Document.

Water Investments

Many developing countries are looking to the World Bank for water investments, and the bank is interested in funding water-related needs. New investments in water management and development are essential for growth in developing countries, and they need to be sustainable—achieving the right balance between water security, and social and environmental protection—said a new World Bank report, Water for Growth and Development, presented at the Forum. "Simply constructing new infrastructure projects is not enough on its own," said Kathy Sierra, World Bank Vice President for Infrastructure. "It is essential to manage and govern water resources effectively. Such water investments will lead to responsible growth, embracing both environmental sustainability and social development."

Public financing for basic water security has been and will remain essential, but the scale of needed investments cannot be provided by public funds alone so the private sector will have an important complementary role to play, said the World Bank report. "All investment, whether public or private, should be complemented by robust regulatory and monitoring frameworks, designed with the active participation of water users and civil society."

But privatization of water is just what many people fear, because the essential liquid could be priced out of their reach.

Some 10,000 people marched in the streets of Mexico City on Saturday [March 18, 2006], demanding that water services not be privatized.

5

The Scarcity of Water Could Lead to War

Roman Kupchinsky

About the Author: *Roman Kupchinsky is the editor of the* Crime, Corruption & Terrorism Watch *weekly published by Radio Free Europe/Radio Liberty, a private, international communications service to eastern and southeastern Europe, Russia, the Caucasus, central Asia, the Middle East, and southwestern Asia, funded by the U.S. Congress.*

Throughout history, access to water has contributed to both domestic and international conflict. The 1967 Six-Day War between Israel and Arab countries actually originated with Israel's decision to divert water from the Jordan River, a river that flows through Israel, Palestine, and Jordan. In this century, water rather than oil may become the world's biggest cause of conflict. The water crisis is likely to hit the hardest in highly populated areas, such as India and China. These countries are already experiencing water shortages, and experts worry that conflicts over water will be the result. Water also has become a major source of concern in central Asia, where the countries of Kyrgyzstan and Tajikistan hold 90 percent of the region's water resources but the area's largest water consumer, Uzbekistan, is located downstream. Similar tensions are arising between Turkey, Syria, and Iraq because Turkey is building a dam to control the flow of the Euphrates River for its agriculture—a project that will likely significantly reduce water to Syria and Iraq. How such conflicts will be

Roman Kupchinsky, "Water Could Become Major Catalyst for Conflict," RadioFree Europe/RadioFreeLiberty, September 16, 2005. Radio Free Europe/Radio Liberty ©

resolved is unclear. One option is called "equitable utilization," which requires nations with water claims to negotiate solutions based on rational concepts such as historical usage, population needs, or other objective factors. Such solutions, however, are very difficult to reach, particularly in regions where political animosities are prevalent, such as the Middle East.

Writing about the 1967 Six Day War in his 2001 memoirs, Israeli Prime Minister Ariel Sharon said that "While the border disputes between Syria and ourselves were of great significance, the matter of water diversion was a stark issue of life and death." "People generally regard 5 June 1967 as the day the Six Day War began," Sharon later told the BBC in 2003. "That is the official date. But, in reality, it started two-and-a-half years earlier, on the day Israel decided to act against the diversion of the Jordan [River]."

Throughout history, access to water has spawned and escalated both domestic and international conflicts. In recent decades, population growth and global warming have both played a major role in raising the demand for and availability of potable water. The U.S. government has predicted that by 2015 almost half of the world's population will be "stressed" for water. Water—rather than oil—could become the world's next biggest catalyst for conflict.

The Water Crunch

In its 2000 "Global Patterns" report, the U.S. Central Intelligence Agency (CIA) predicted that, by the year 2015, "nearly half the world's population—more than 3 billion people—will live in countries which are 'water stressed.'" According to the report, that means their populations will have less than 1,700 cubic meters each of water per year, generally considered the minimal threshold for acceptable living standards. The water crunch will make itself felt most on food supplies. Agriculture is the world's biggest user of water—it takes at least 2,000 liters to produce enough food for one person for one day. That translates into 730,000 liters annually per person.

A water crisis would likely impact hardest on the world's most heavily populated regions such as China and India. Those countries are also some of the world's fastest-growing economies and are also caught in a squeeze for energy resources. India, according to the CIA report, will become severely starved for water by 2015. And the competition with Pakistan for water in Kashmir has contributed to an ongoing conflict in the region.

Experts worry that dwindling water supplies could likely result in regional conflicts in the future.

In northern China, close to the Russian border, the water table beneath some of the major grain-producing regions is falling by 1.52 meters every year. Northern China, according to the Worldwatch Institute website (http://www.world watch.org), "is home to roughly 43 percent of China's population but has only 14 percent of China's water resources. China's annual per capita water resources of 2,292 cubic meters [1.86 acre feet] are one of the lowest levels in the world, only slightly above that of India. North China's per capita water resources, at 750 cubic meters per year, are a fraction of China's already low figure."

Source of Tension

Experts worry that dwindling water supplies could likely result in regional conflicts in the future. For example, in oil-and-gas rich Central Asia, the upstream countries of Kyrgyzstan and Tajikistan hold 90 percent of the region's water resources, while Uzbekistan, the largest consumer of water in the region, is located downstream.

Water has also become a major source of tension between Turkey, Syria, and Iraq. Turkey, located upstream of the Tigris and Euphrates river systems, began the Southeast Anatolia

(GAP) Project in 1990, which will give it extensive control over the flow of Euphrates water and is expected to double Turkey's irrigated farmland. The project is expected to be completed by 2010. In an article, "The New Water Politics Of The Middle East" (*Strategic Review*, Summer 1999), the authors explain that: "Despite the signing of a protocol ensuring Syrian access to Euphrates water in 1987, Turkish development efforts have increasingly threatened to marginalize and even eliminate Syrian access to water." "In the future," the article continues, "Turkish-Syrian disputes over water could escalate into regional conflict. . . . Once fully operational, the GAP Project may reduce Euphrates water to Syria by 40 percent and Iraq by up to 80 percent. Such activity, critical for Syria, will also be significant enough to substantially affect Iraq."

Local water conflicts also have the potential to escalate, especially in states with weak central government. According to a September report from RFE/RL's [Radio Free Europe/Radio Liberty] Radio Free Afghanistan, the head of the Chardara District, in northern Afghanistan, has allowed water from an irrigation canal, which serves some 25,000 hect[ares] of land, to be used to irrigate rice fields upstream of the canal. The amount of water needed for rice paddies is far greater than for normal irrigation and the farmers downstream were subsequently faced with a water shortage. The district chief ignored the needs of the downstream farmers and the government failed to intervene.

Looking for a Solution

Such scenarios are not uncommon. How such potential conflicts can be resolved is a problem facing international organizations and security experts, especially when states often tend to interpret international law differently. According to a 1999 article in the *UNESCO Courier*, "Custom-Built Solutions For International Disputes," by Joseph W. Dellapenna, a professor of international law, there is international agreement that "only riparian nations—nations across which, or along which, a river flows—have any legal right, apart from an agreement, to use the water of a river." Dellapenna continues: "Beyond that, however, there are two types of international claim. The upper-riparian nations initially base their claims on absolute territorial sovereignty, typically claiming the right to do whatever they choose with the water regardless of its effect on other riparian nations. Downstream nations, on the other hand, generally make a claim to the absolute integrity of the river, insisting that upper-riparian nations can do nothing that affects the quantity or quality of water flowing."

Dellapenna points out that "the usual solution" to disputed claims over water is known as "equitable utilization," where each nation recognizes the rights of others to use water from the same source. "Under this principle, countries usually decide on how much water is allocated to one state or another by looking for some more or less objective standard such as historic patterns of use or the amount of land that could be irrigated in each nation. They also take into account 'objective' factors, like the need for more water for growing populations." In theory, "equitable utilization" is a rational solution—in practice however, problems arise, especially where water disputes are exacerbated by political animosity. In the case of the Middle East, specialists believe that water agreements will be hard to achieve without solutions to political conflicts.

6

The Water Crisis Does Not Have to Lead to War

Aaron T. Wolf, Annika Kramer, Alexander Carius, and Geoffrey D. Dabelko

About the Authors: *Aaron T. Wolf is associate professor of Geography in the Department of Geosciences at Oregon State University and Ddirector of the Transboundary Freshwater Dispute Database. Annika Kramer is research fellow and Alexander Carius is director of Adelphi Research in Berlin. Geoffrey D. Dabelko is the director of the Environmental Change and Security Project at the Woodrow Wilson International Center for Scholars in Washington, D.C.*

Because of the impending water crisis, wars over water seem imminent, especially since conflicts over water have occurred throughout history. However, no nations have ever gone to war over water and most international water disputes have been settled peacefully. This is because water is so important that nations cannot afford to fight over it. Indeed, water has more often created a pathway to peace, even between warring countries. Water negotiations were held between Cambodia, Laos, Thailand, and Vietnam during the Vietnam War; Israel and Jordan held water talks for years when they were officially at war; and southern African countries signed a number of water agreements during a series of wars in the 1970s and 1980s. Today, more than ever, it is necessary to stop predicting war and pursue peace. The basic foundation for peacemaking is good gover-

Aaron T. Wolf, Annika Kramer, Alexander Carius, and Geoffrey D. Dabelko, "Water Can Be a Pathway to Peace, Not War," *Worldwatch Institute*, June 2005. © 2005 World Watch, www.worldwatch.org. Reproduced by permission.

nance—the lack of corruption—and money, but a variety of
other strategies are also necessary. By definition, water management is conflict management, but cooperative water management can be used to head off conflict and promote peace among
nations.

"Water wars are coming!" the newspaper headlines
scream. It seems obvious—rivalries over water have
been the source of disputes since humans settled down to
cultivate food. Even our language reflects these ancient roots:
"rivalry" comes from the Latin rivalis, or "one using the
same river as another." Countries or provinces bordering
the same river (known as "riparians") are often rivals for the
water they share. As the number of international river basins
(and impact of water scarcity) has grown so do the warnings
that these countries will take up arms to ensure their access to
water. In 1995, for example, World Bank Vice President Ismail
Serageldin claimed that "the wars of the next century will be
about water."

No Wars over Water

These apocalyptic warnings fly in the face of history: no nations have gone to war specifically over water resources for
thousands of years. International water disputes—even among
fierce enemies—are resolved peacefully, even as conflicts erupt
over other issues. In fact, instances of cooperation between riparian nations outnumbered conflicts by more than two to
one between 1945 and 1999. Why? Because water is so important, nations cannot afford to fight over it. Instead, water fuels
greater interdependence. By coming together to jointly manage their shared water resources, countries build trust and
prevent conflict. Water can be a negotiating tool, too: it can
offer a communication lifeline connecting countries in the
midst of crisis. Thus, by crying "water wars," doomsayers ignore a promising way to help prevent war: cooperative water
resources management.

Of course, people compete—sometimes violently—for water. Within a nation, users—farmers, hydroelectric dams, recreational users, environmentalists—are often at odds, and the probability of a mutually acceptable solution falls as the number of stakeholders rises. Water is never the single—and hardly ever the major—cause of conflict. But it can exacerbate existing tensions. History is littered with examples of violent water conflicts: just as Californian farmers bombed pipelines moving water from Owens Valley to Los Angeles in the early 1900s, Chinese farmers in Shandong clashed with police in 2000 to protest government plans to divert irrigation water to cities and industries. But these conflicts usually break out within nations. International rivers are a different story.

The world's 263 international river basins cover 45.3 percent of Earth's land surface, host about 40 percent of the world's population, and account for approximately 60 percent of global river flow. And the number is growing, largely due to the "internationalization" of basins through political changes like the breakup of the Soviet Union, as well as improved mapping technology. Strikingly, territory in 145 nations falls within international basins, and 33 countries are located almost entirely within these basins. As many as 17 countries share one river basin, the Danube [a river in Europe].

International cooperation around water has a long and successful history; some of the world's most vociferous enemies have negotiated water agreements.

Contrary to received wisdom, evidence proves this interdependence does not lead to war. Researchers at Oregon State University compiled a dataset of every reported interaction (conflictive or cooperative) between two or more nations that was driven by water in the last half century. They found that the rate of cooperation overwhelms the incidence of acute

conflict. In the last 50 years, only 37 disputes involved violence, and 30 of those occurred between Israel and one of its
neighbors. Outside of the Middle East, researchers found only
5 violent events while 157 treaties were negotiated and signed.
The total number of water-related events between nations also
favors cooperation: the 1,228 cooperative events dwarf the 507
conflict-related events. Despite the fiery rhetoric of politi-
cians—aimed more often at their own constituencies than at
the enemy—most actions taken over water are mild. Of all the
events, 62 percent are verbal, and more than two-thirds of
these were not official statements.

A History of Cooperation

Simply put, water is a greater pathway to peace than conflict
in the world's international river basins. International cooperation around water has a long and successful history; some
of the world's most vociferous enemies have negotiated water
agreements. The institutions they have created are resilient,
even when relations are strained. The Mekong Committee, for
example, established by Cambodia, Laos, Thailand, and Viet
Nam in 1957, exchanged data and information on the river
basin throughout the Viet Nam War.

Israel and Jordan held secret "picnic table" talks to manage
the Jordan River since 1953, even though they were officially
at war from 1948 until the 1994 treaty. The Indus River Commission survived two major wars between India and Pakistan.
And all 10 Nile Basin riparian countries are currently involved
in senior government-level negotiations to develop the basin
cooperatively, despite the verbal battles conducted in the me-
dia. Riparians will endure such tough, protracted negotiations
to ensure access to this essential resource and its economic
and social benefits.

Southern African countries signed a number of river basin
agreements while the region was embroiled in a series of wars
in the 1970s and 1980s, including the "people's war" in South

Africa and civil wars in Mozambique and Angola. These complex negotiations produced rare moments of peaceful cooperation. Now that most of the wars and the apartheid era have ended, water management forms one of the foundations for cooperation in the region, producing one of the first protocols signed within the Southern African Development Community (SADC).

Time for Peacemaking

Today, more than ever, it is time to stop propagating threats of "water wars" and aggressively pursue a water peacemaking strategy. Why?

- "Water wars" warnings force the military and other security groups to take over negotiations and push out development partners, like aid agencies and international financial institutions.

- Water management offers an avenue for peaceful dialogue between nations, even when combatants are fighting over other issues.

- Water cooperation forges people-to-people or expert-to-expert connections, as demonstrated by the transboundary water and sanitation projects Friends of the Earth Middle East conducts in Israel, Jordan, and Palestine.

- A water peacemaking strategy can create shared regional identities and institutionalize cooperation on issues larger than water, as exemplified by the formation of SADC in post-apartheid southern Africa.

Strategies for Peace

Good governance—the lack of corruption—is the basic foundation for the success of any agreement. Obviously, money is also a big challenge. But good governance and money are not enough. Several policy initiatives could help peacemakers use water to build peace:

1. Identify and utilize more experienced facilitators who are perceived as truly neutral. The World Bank's success facilitating the Nile Basin Initiative suggests they have skills worth replicating in other basins.

2. Be willing to support a long process that might not produce quick or easily measurable results. Sweden's 20-year commitment to Africa's Great Lakes region is a model to emulate. Typical project cycles—often governed by shifting government administrations or political trends—are not long enough.

3. Ensure that the riparians themselves drive the process. Riparian nations require funders and facilitators who do not dominate the process and claim all the glory. Strengthening less powerful riparians' negotiating skills can help prevent disputes, as can strengthening the capacity of excluded, marginalized, or weaker groups to articulate their interests.

4. Strengthen water resource management. Capacity building—to generate and analyze data, develop sustainable water management plans, use conflict resolution techniques, or encourage stakeholder participation—should target water management institutions, local nongovernmental organizations, water users' associations, and religious groups.

5. Balance the benefits of closed-door, high-level negotiations with the benefits of including all stakeholders—NGOs [nongovernmental organizations], farmers, indigenous groups—throughout the process. Preventing severe conflicts requires informing or explicitly consulting all relevant stakeholders before making management decisions. Without such extensive and regular public participation, stakeholders might reject projects out of hand.

Cooperative Water Management

Water management is, by definition, conflict management. For all the twenty-first century wizardry—dynamic modeling, remote sensing, geographic information systems, desalination, biotechnology, or demand management—and the new-found concern with globalization and privatization, the crux of water disputes is still little more than opening a diversion gate or garbage floating downstream. Obviously, there are no guarantees that the future will look like the past; water and conflict are undergoing slow but steady changes. An unprecedented number of people lack access to a safe, stable supply of water. Two to five million people die each year from water-related illness. Water use is shifting to less traditional sources such as deep fossil aquifers and wastewater reclamation. Conflict, too, is becoming less traditional, driven increasingly by internal or local pressures or, more subtly, by poverty and instability. These changes suggest that tomorrow's water disputes may look very different from today's.

No matter what the future holds, we do not need violent conflict to prove water is a matter of life and death. Water—being international, indispensable, and emotional—can serve as a cornerstone for confidence building and a potential entry point for peace. More research could help identify exactly how water best contributes to cooperation. With this, cooperative water resources management could be used more effectively to head off conflict and to support sustainable peace among nations.

7

The Risks of Privatization Must Be Balanced by Government Oversight

Peter H. Gleick, Gary Wolff, Elizabeth L. Chalecki, and Rachel Reyes

About the Authors: *Peter H. Gleick is an internationally-recognized water expert and cofounder of the Pacific Institute for Studies in Development, Environment, and Security, an independent research and policy organization that focuses on sustainable development, environmental protection and international security. Gary Wolff is the Institute's principal economist and engineer, and Elizabeth L. Chalecki and Rachel Reyes, at the time of this report, were research associates at the organization.*

Recent ideas in the debate about water suggest [it] should be considered an economic good, subject to market forces and managed by private companies. The rush toward privatization, however, has failed to take into account the social, cultural, and ecological values of water. Water can and should be both a social and an economic good. Yet globalization threatens to take water away from local environments and people, and international rules and treaties do not yet provide adequate protection. One of the most controversial trends is the transfer of water services

Peter H. Gleick, Gary Wolff, Elizabeth Chalecki, and Rachel Reyes, "The New Economy of Water: The Risks and Benefits of Globalization and Privatization of Fresh Water, Executive Summary," The Pacific Institute for Studies in Development, Environment and Security, February 2002. © 2002 Pacific Institute. Reproduced by permission.

from public entities to private companies, a result pushed by the World Bank and other international agencies. This trend has created growing opposition from local communities and has sometimes resulted in violent protests by those who fear that private corporations will only seek profits and not provide for people's water needs. In fact, the risks of privatization are many and can only be balanced by strong governments that are able to provide water services equitably. Despite the strong opposition, however, public-private partnerships in water supply are likely to increase. It is therefore necessary to follow certain principles, so that water will continue to be managed as a social good, using sound economics and strong government regulation and oversight. Water is too important to be left entirely to the private sector.

New voices are beginning to be heard in the debate over water, and new ideas—good and bad—considered. Among the most powerful and controversial of these new ideas is that water should be considered an economic good— subject to the rules and power of markets, multinational corporations, and international trading regimes.

In the last decade, this idea has been put into practice in dozens of ways, in hundreds of places, affecting millions of people. Prices have been set for water previously provided for free. Private companies have been invited to take over the management, operation, and sometimes even the ownership of public water systems. Commercial trade in bottled water has boomed. International development agencies that used to work with governments to improve water services are now pushing privatization efforts. Proposals have been floated to transfer fresh water in bulk across international borders and even across oceans. This paper addresses these issues and concerns, and offers principles and standards to guide policymakers in the future.

Privatization Must Be Implemented Carefully

We do not think the trend toward globalization and privatization of fresh water can be stopped, nor do we think it has to be. In some places and in some circumstances, letting private companies take responsibility for some aspects of water provision or management may help millions of poor people receive access to basic water services.

However, there is little doubt that the headlong rush toward private markets has failed to address some of the most important issues and concerns about water. In particular, water has vital social, cultural, and ecological roles to play that cannot be protected by purely market forces. In addition, certain management goals and social values require direct and strong government support and protection. Some of the consequences of privatization may be irreversible; hence they deserve special scrutiny and control.

There is little doubt that the headlong rush toward private markets has failed to address some of the most important issues and concerns about water.

As a result, we conclude that any efforts to privatize or commodify water must be evaluated far more carefully than they have been. Privatization efforts should be accompanied by guarantees to respect certain principles and support specific social objectives. Among these are the need to provide for the basic water needs of people and ecosystems, permit equitable access to water for poor populations, include affected parties in decision making, and improve water-use efficiency and productivity. Openness, transparency, and strong public regulatory oversight are fundamental requirements in any efforts to shift the public responsibility for providing clean water to private entities.

Water Is Both a Social Good and an Economic Good

Water can be both a social and an economic good. Access to clean water is fundamental to survival and critical for reducing the prevalence of many water-related diseases. Other dimensions of water supply also have a social good character and therefore require governmental action, oversight, or regulation. Because water is important to the process of economic development, essential for life and health, and has cultural or religious significance, it has often been provided at subsidized prices or for free in many situations. In theory, though not always in practice, this makes water available to even the poorest segments of society.

Frustration over the failure to meet basic needs for water for all people in the last century has led to a rethinking of national and international water priorities and policies. Among these is the potential value of applying economic tools and principles. The International Conference on Water and Environment, held in Dublin, Ireland in January 1992, concluded, among other things, that: "Water has an economic value in all its competing uses and should be recognized as an economic good." Following the Dublin meeting, the United Nations Conference on Environment and Development (held in Rio in 1992) clearly recognized that economics must play a part in efficient water management: "Integrated water resources management is based on the perception of water as an integral part of the ecosystem, a natural resource, and a social and economic good."

What has been far less clear is how, practically, to achieve the right balance between managing water as an economic and a social good. This has become evident in the growing debate over globalization and privatization of water worldwide.

Globalization and International Trade in Water

The world's water is unevenly distributed, with great natural variations in abundance. Indeed, the complex and expensive water systems that have been built over the past few centuries have been designed to capture water in wet periods for use in droughts and to move water from water-rich regions to water-poor regions. As domestic, industrial, and agricultural demands for fresh water have grown, entrepreneurs have created a wide range of markets for water, leading to various forms of international water trading and exchanges.

In the past, most large-scale transfers of water occurred within national and political borders. Agreements were also common among nations that share a watershed, such as the U.S. and Mexico over the Colorado, the Sudan and Egypt over the Nile, and many others. Now, however, proposals for bulk water transfers are being made at international, and even global, levels between parties that do not share a watershed. In recent years Alaskan, Canadian, Icelandic, Malaysian, Turkish, and other waters have been proposed as sources for international trade in bulk water. Besides the historically important environmental and socioeconomic implications of water transfers, the possibility of large-scale bulk trading of fresh water has now become an issue in international trade negotiations and disputes.

The possibility of bulk water transfers has caused concern in water-abundant regions that a global water-trading regime might lead to the requirement that abundant resources be tapped to provide fresh water for the rest of the world, at the expense of local environment and people.

The Rules: International Trading Regimes

Rules governing international trade, such as those set out by GATT [General Agreement on Tariffs and Trade], WTO [World Trade Organization], and NAFTA [North American

Free Trade Agreement], are complex and often contradictory. In recent years, efforts to implement standard rules have been developed in various international forums, and these rules have become increasingly sophisticated and important to the global economy. At the same time, they have become increasingly controversial, as their implications for the environment, civil society, and local economies become clearer.

There is little legal precedent pertaining directly to international trade in water, making it difficult to predict the outcomes of current and future trade disputes in this area with certainty. However, commercial pressures to export water are increasing, making resolution of these ambiguities an important goal. In addition, adverse, even virulent public sentiment over several proposed exports highlights the need to resolve and clarify issues.

There is considerable debate among legal experts as to whether WTO member governments can control, limit, or regulate bulk water exports, and there are few legal precedents. We believe a strong argument can be made to support banning bulk exports of water under GATT Article XX(g) where freshwater water resources are "non-renewable" or exhaustible through overuse or abuse, assuming domestic production or consumption is also limited to prevent nonrenewable uses. In some circumstances, we also believe that GATT would support a ban on bulk exports of water when such exports threaten ecosystems or human health.

Our analysis also suggests, however, that profitable largescale, long-term bulk exports of water across international borders are unlikely for many reasons, especially the high economic cost of moving water. Nevertheless, great uncertainty continues to revolve around the legal interpretation of international trade agreements in the context of globalizing water resources and we urge clarification of rules governing bulk exports of water. In particular, we recommend national water policies that explicitly protect water necessary to support human and ecosystem health and prohibit the mining and export of non-renewable water resources.

The New Economy of Water: Privatization

One of the most important—and controversial—trends in the global water arena is the accelerating transfer of the production, distribution, or management of water or water services from public entities into private hands—a process loosely called "privatization." Treating water as an economic good, and privatizing water systems, are not new ideas. Private entrepreneurs, investor-owned utilities, or other market tools have long provided water or water services in different parts of the world. What is new is the extent of privatization efforts underway today, and the growing public awareness of, and attention to, problems associated with these efforts.

There is rapidly growing opposition to privatization proposals from local community groups, unions, human rights organizations, and even public water providers.

The issue has resurfaced for several reasons: first, public water agencies have been unable to satisfy the most basic needs for water for all humans; second, major multinational corporations have greatly expanded their efforts to take over responsibility for a larger portion of the water service market than ever before; and third, several recent highly publicized privatization efforts have failed or generated great controversy.

The privatization of water encompasses an enormous variety of possible water-management arrangements. Privatization can be partial, leading to so-called public/private partnerships, or complete, leading to the total elimination of government responsibility for water systems. At the largest scale, private water companies build, own, and operate water systems around the world with annual revenues of approximately $300 billion, excluding revenues for sales of bottled water. At the smallest scale, private water vendors and sales of water at small kiosks and shops provide many more individuals and families with basic water supplies than they did 30 years ago. Taken all together, the growing roles and responsibilities of the private sector have important and poorly understood implications for water and human well-being.

As a measure of the new importance of privatization, the World Bank, other international aid agencies, and some water organizations like the World Water Council are increasingly pushing privatization in their efforts, but without a common set of guidelines and principles. As a result, there is rapidly growing opposition to privatization proposals from local community groups, unions, human rights organizations, and even public water providers.

Protests—sometimes violent—have occurred in many places, including Bolivia, Paraguay, South Africa, the Philippines, and various globalization conferences around the world. Opposition arises from concerns over the economic implications of privatizing water resources, the risks to ecosystems, the power of corporate players, foreign control over a fundamental natural resource, inequities of access to water, and the exclusion of communities from decisions about their own resources. Some fundamental principles are necessary to prevent inequitable, uneconomic, and environmentally damaging privatization agreements.

The Risks of Privatization: Can and Will They Be Managed?

The move toward privatization of water services raises many concerns, and in some places, even violent opposition. In large part, opposition arises because of doubts about whether purely private markets can address the many different social good aspects of water, or whether some non-market mechanisms are necessary to serve social objectives. Other concerns relate to a fundamental distrust of corporate players and worries about the transfer of profits and assets outside of a community or even a country. The greatest need for water services often exists in those countries with the weakest public sectors; yet the greatest risks of failed privatization also exist where governments are weak. The rapid pace of privatization in recent years and the inappropriate ways several projects have been implemented have compounded the worries of local communities, non-governmental organizations, and policymakers. As a result, private water companies are increasingly seeing serious and sustained public opposition to privatization proposals.

Water Provision is a Basic Responsibility of Governments Governments have a fundamental duty to see that basic services, such as water, sewerage, and energy, are provided to their people. The failure to satisfy such basic needs, or at least provide the means to do so, must be viewed as irresponsible. Efforts of international lending agencies and development organizations have, in the past, focused on helping governments to provide these services. More recently, these organizations have begun to shift their efforts, pushing privatization as a new solution. We have serious concerns about this transfer of responsibility and the loss of control it implies.

Privatization May Bypass Under-Represented and Under-Served Communities One of the basic goals of any proposal to provide water services (publicly or privately) should be to meet explicitly the needs of under-served communities through an expansion of access to water or wastewater services. Poor peri-urban populations have traditionally been under-served because they lack political power or representation, they come from unofficial "communities," or they may be unable to pay as much for water as residents in wealthier areas. Privatization can potentially worsen this neglect.

Privatization Can Worsen Economic Inequities and the Affordability of Water One of the leading arguments offered by proponents of privatization is that private management or ownership of water systems can reduce the water prices paid by consumers. Ironically, one of the greatest concerns of local communities is that privatization will lead to higher costs for water and water services. The actual record is mixed—both results have occurred. One of the potential benefits of privatization is elimination of inappropriate subsidies. We note, however, that lack of water subsidies in some cases can have disastrous results, especially when combined with pressures to recover costs. There has been inadequate attention given in privatization negotiations and debates to identifying the difference between appropriate and inappropriate subsidies. When water systems or operations are privatized, it may be desirable to protect some groups of citizens or businesses from paying the full cost of service.

Privatization Agreements May Fail to Protect Public Ownership of Water and Water Rights Privatization of water management can, under some circumstances, lead to the loss of local ownership of water systems, which in turn can lead to neglect of the public interest. Many of the concerns expressed about privatization relate to the control of water rights and changes in water allocations, rather than explicit financial or economic problems. In part, this is the result of the deep feelings people have for water. It is also the result, however, of serious neglect of these issues by some who promote privatization.

Privatization Agreements Often Fail to Include Public Participation and Contract Monitoring Oversight and monitoring of public-private agreements are key public responsibilities. Far more effort has been spent trying to ease financial constraints and government oversight, and to promote private-sector involvement, than to define broad guidelines for public access and oversight, monitor the public interest, and ensure public participation and transparency. Weaknesses in monitoring progress can lead to ineffective service provision, discriminatory behavior, or violations of water-quality protections.

Inappropriate Privatization Efforts Ignore Impacts on Ecosystems or Downstream Water Users Many privatization contracts include provisions to encourage the development of new water supplies, often over a long period of time. If privatization contracts do not also guarantee ecosystem water requirements, development of new supply options will undermine ecosystem health and well-being (for both public and private developments). Balancing ecological needs with water supply, hydroelectric power, and downstream uses of water is a complex task involving many stakeholders.

Privatization Efforts May Neglect the Potential for Water-Use Efficiency and Conservation Improvements One of the greatest concerns of privatization watchdogs is that efficiency programs are typically ignored or even cancelled after authority for managing public systems is turned over to private entities. Improvements in efficiency reduce water sales, and hence may lower revenues. As a result, utilities or companies that provide utility services may have little or no financial incentive to encourage conservation. In addition, conservation is often less capital intensive and therefore creates fewer opportunities for investors. Consequently, it may be neglected in comparison with traditional, centralized water-supply projects.

Privatization Agreements May Lessen Protection of Water Quality Private suppliers of water have few economic incentives to address long-term health problems associated with low levels of some pollutants. In addition, private water suppliers have an incentive to understate or misrepresent to customers the size and potential impacts of problems that do occur. As a result, there is widespread agreement that maintaining strong regulatory oversight is a necessary component of protecting water quality. When strong regulatory oversight exists, privatization can lead to improvements in water quality.

Privatization Agreements Often Lack Dispute-Resolution Procedures Public water companies are usually subject to political dispute-resolution processes involving local stakeholders. Privatized water systems are subject to legal processes that involve non-local stakeholders and perhaps non-local levels of the legal system. This change in who resolves disputes, and the rules for dispute resolution, is accompanied by increased potential for political conflicts over privatization agreements. While we strongly support the concept of standards, benchmarks, and clear contract agreements, such standards must be negotiated in an open, transparent process, with input from all parties, not just water companies.

Privatization of Water Systems May be Irreversible When governments transfer control over their water system to private companies, the loss of internal skills and expertise may be irreversible, or nearly so. Many contracts are long term—for as much as 10 to 20 years. Management expertise, engineering knowledge, and other assets in the public domain may be lost for good. Indeed, while there is growing experience with the transfer of such assets to private hands, there is little or no recent experience with the public sector re-acquiring such assets from the private sector.

The Need for Strong Governments

We believe that the responsibility for providing water and water services should still rest with local communities and governments, and that efforts should be made to strengthen the ability of governments to meet water needs. As described in this study, the potential advantages of privatization are often greatest where governments have been weakest and failed to meet basic water needs. Where strong governments are able to provide water services effectively and equitably, the attractions of privatization decrease substantially. Unfortunately, the worst risks of privatization are also where governments are weakest, where they are unable to provide the oversight and management functions necessary to protect public interests. This contradiction poses the greatest challenge for those who hope to make privatization work successfully.

Despite the vociferous, and often justified, opposition to water privatization, proposals for public-private partnerships in water supply and management are likely to become more numerous in the future. We do not argue here that privatization efforts must stop. We do, however, argue that all privatization agreements should meet certain standards and incorporate specific principles. Consequently, we offer the following Principles and Standards for privatization of water-supply systems and infrastructure.

Continue to Manage Water as a Social Good

1.1 *Meet basic human needs for water. All residents in a service area should be guaranteed a basic water quantity under any privatization agreement.* Contract agreements to provide water services in any region must ensure that unmet basic human water needs are met first, before more water is provided to existing customers. Basic water requirements should be clearly defined.

1.2 *Meet basic ecosystem needs for water.* Natural ecosystems should be guaranteed a basic water requirement under any privatization agreement. Basic water-supply protections for natural ecosystems must be put in place in every region of the world. Such protections should be written into every privatization agreement, enforced by government oversight.

1.3 *The basic water requirement for users should be provided at subsidized rates when necessary for reasons of poverty.* Subsidies should not be encouraged blindly, but some subsidies for specific groups of people or industries are occasionally justified. One example is subsidies for meeting basic water requirements when that minimum amount of water cannot be paid for due to poverty.

Use Sound Economics in Water Management

2.1 *Water and water services should be provided at fair and reasonable rates.* Provision of water and water services should not be free. Appropriate subsidies should be evaluated and discussed in public. Rates should be designed to encourage efficient and effective use of water.

2.2. *Whenever possible, link proposed rate increases with agreed-upon improvements in service.* Experience has shown that water users are often willing to pay for improvements in service when such improvements are designed with their participation and when improvements are actually delivered. Even when rate increases are primarily motivated by cost increases, linking the rate increase to improvements in service creates a performance incentive for the water supplier and increases the value of water and water services to users.

2.3 *Subsidies, if necessary, should be economically and socially sound.* Subsidies are not all equal from an economic point of view. For example, subsidies to low-income users that do not reduce the price of water are more appropriate than those that do because lower water prices encourage inefficient water use. Similarly, mechanisms should be instituted to regularly review and eliminate subsidies that no longer serve an appropriate social purpose.

2.4 *Private companies should be required to demonstrate that new water-supply projects are less expensive than projects to improve water conservation and water-use efficiency before they are permitted to invest and raise water rates to repay the investment.* Privatization agreements should not permit new supply projects unless such projects can be proven to be less costly than improving the efficiency of existing water distribution and use. When considered seriously, water-efficiency investments can earn an equal or higher rate of return to that earned by new water-supply investments. Rate structures should permit companies to earn a return on efficiency and conservation investments.

Maintain Strong Government Regulation and Oversight

3.1 *Governments should retain or establish public ownership or control of water sources.* The "social good" dimensions of water cannot be fully protected if ownership of water sources is entirely private. Permanent and unequivocal public ownership of water sources gives the public the strongest single point of leverage in ensuring that an acceptable balance between social and economic concerns is achieved.

3.2 *Public agencies and water-service providers should monitor water quality.* Governments should define and enforce water-quality laws. Water suppliers cannot effectively regulate water quality. Although this point has been recognized in many privatization decisions, government water-quality regulators are often under-informed and under-funded, leaving public decisions about water quality in private hands. Governments should define and enforce laws and regulations. Government agencies or independent watchdogs should monitor, and publish information on, water quality. Where governments are weak, formal and explicit mechanisms to protect water quality must be even stronger.

3.3 *Contracts that lay out the responsibilities of each partner are a prerequisite for the success of any privatization.* Contracts must protect the public interest; this requires provisions ensuring the quality of service and a regulatory regime that is transparent, accessible, and accountable to the public. Good contracts will include explicit performance criteria and standards, with oversight by government regulatory agencies and non-governmental organizations.

3.4 *Clear dispute-resolution procedures should be developed prior to privatization.* Dispute resolution procedures should be specified clearly in contracts. It is necessary to develop practical procedures that build upon local institutions and practices, are free of corruption, and difficult to circumvent.

3.5 *Independent technical assistance and contract review should be standard.* Weaker governments are most vulnerable to the risk of being forced into accepting weak contracts. Many of the problems associated with privatization have resulted from inadequate contract review or ambiguous contract language. In principle, many of these problems can be avoided by requiring advance independent technical and contract review.

3.6 *Negotiations over privatization contracts should be open, transparent, and include all affected stakeholders.* Numerous political and financial problems for water customers and private companies have resulted from arrangements that were perceived as corrupt or not in the best interests of the public. Stakeholder participation is widely recognized as the best way of avoiding these problems. Broad participation by affected parties ensures that diverse values and varying viewpoints are articulated and incorporated into the process. It also provides a sense of ownership and stewardship over the process and resulting decisions. We recommend the creation of public advisory committees with broad community representation to advise governments proposing privatization; formal public review of contracts in advance of signing agreements; and public education efforts in advance of any transfer of public responsibilities to private companies. International agency or charitable foundation funding of technical support to these committees should be provided.

Privatization Must Be Balanced with Social Values

As the 21st century unfolds, complex and new ideas will be tested, modified, and put in place to oversee the world's growing economic, cultural, and political connections. One of the most powerful and controversial will be new ways of managing the global economy. Even in the first years of the new century, political conflict over the new economy has been front and center in the world's attention.

Letting private companies take responsibility for managing some aspects of water services has the potential to help millions of poor receive access to basic water services.

This controversy extends to how fresh water is to be obtained, managed, and provided to the world's people. In the water community, the concept of water as an "economic good" has become the focal point of contention. In the last decade, the idea that fresh water should be increasingly subject to the rules and power of markets, prices, and international trading regimes has been put into practice in dozens of ways, in hundreds of places, affecting millions of people. Prices have been set for water previously provided for free. Private corporations are taking control of the management, operation, and sometimes even the ownership of previously public water systems. Sales of bottled water are booming. Proposals have been floated to transfer large quantities of fresh water across international borders, and even across oceans.

These ideas and trends have generated enormous controversy. In some places and in some circumstances, treating water as an economic good can offer major advantages in the battle to provide every human with their basic water requirements, while protecting natural ecosystems. Letting private companies take responsibility for managing some aspects of water services has the potential to help millions of poor receive access to basic water services. But in the past decade, the trend toward privatization of water has greatly accelerated, with both successes and spectacular failures. Insufficient effort has been made to understand the risks and limitations of water privatization, and to put in place guiding principles and standards to govern privatization efforts.

There is little doubt that the headlong rush toward private markets has failed to address some of the most important issues and concerns about water. In particular, water has vital social, cultural, and ecological roles to play that cannot be protected by purely market forces. In addition, certain management goals and social values require direct and strong government support and protection, yet privatization efforts are increasing rapidly in regions where strong governments do not exist.

We strongly recommend that any efforts to privatize or commodify water be accompanied by formal guarantees to respect certain principles and support specific social objectives. Among these are the need to provide for the basic water needs of humans and ecosystems as a top priority. Also important is ensuring independent monitoring and enforcement of water quality standards, equitable access to water for poor populations, inclusion of all affected parties in decision making, and increased reliance on water-use efficiency and productivity improvements. Openness, transparency, and strong public regulatory oversight are fundamental requirements in any efforts to share the public responsibility for providing clean water to private entities.

Water is both an economic and social good. As a result, unregulated market forces can never completely and equitably satisfy social objectives. Given the legitimate concerns about the risks of this "new economy of water," efforts to capture the benefits of the private sector must be balanced with efforts to address its flaws. Water is far too important to the well being of humans and our environment to be placed entirely in the private sector.

8

Privatization Has Failed to Address the Water Problem in Developing Nations

John Vidal

About the Author*: John Vidal is the environment editor for the* Guardian, *a long-running and respected British newspaper.*

A 2006 report by the United Nations (UN) indicates that political opposition to the privatization of water resources is causing many major multinational corporations that have taken over water supplies to pull out of developing countries, either voluntarily or involuntarily. The political resistance, and sometimes violence, has often been in response to their decisions to raise the prices of water. Thames Water, for example, is leaving Shanghai, China; Saur is leaving Mozambique and Zimbabwe; and Suez is downsizing in Latin America. Major demonstrations have also been faced by European and American companies in Bolivia, Malaysia, South Africa, and Indonesia. Water privatization was seen by the World Bank and developed nations as the most effective way to provide clean water to poor countries, but so far the rich have benefited at the expense of the poor. While some companies seem to have been successful, many have faced accusations of profiteering or failing to provide water to poor communities. The UN report concludes that the trend of water privatization is reversing. Local and smaller water companies are now entering the field, but their abilities to improve water supply are untested, so it is time for governments to again become more involved. Development groups welcomed the news because they believe privatization in developing countries has failed.

Millions of people could have to wait years for clean water as some of the world's largest companies pull out of developing countries because of growing doubts about privatisation projects, a major UN [United Nations] report reveals today [March 22, 2006]. Political and consumer unease about multimillion-pound schemes that were intended to end the cycle of drought and death that has afflicted many countries is forcing major multinationals to think again. "Due to the political and high-risk operations, many multinational water companies are decreasing their activities in developing countries," says the UN's second world water development report, published today [March 22, 2006] in Mexico City. . . . "In many settings, privatisation is a heavily politicised issue that is creating social and political discontent and sometimes outright violence."

Many companies have met intense political resistance in the past five years after winning large contracts to supply cities but then having to raise prices significantly. Some have been forced out of countries, others have left voluntarily. The report cites Thames Water leaving Shanghai [China], Saur leaving Mozambique and Zimbabwe, and Suez downsizing in Latin America and Africa, as well as major demonstrations against European and American water companies in Bolivia, Malaysia, South Africa and Indonesia. Many companies, it says, have not been able to make money and are now concentrating on less risky markets in Europe and North America.

Benefits to the Rich at the Expense of the Poor

Water privatisation was seen by the World Bank and G8 countries [Canada, France, Germany, Italy, Japan, Russia, the United Kingdom, and the United States] as the most effective way to bring clean water to large numbers of poor countries throughout the 1990s, but in spite of investments of $25bn [billion] (£14bn) between 1990 and 1997, the rich have mostly benefited at the expense of the poor. Sub-Saharan Africa has received less than 1% of all the money invested in water supplies by private companies in the last 10 years. "Those who have benefited from private water services in developing countries are predominantly those living in relatively affluent urban pockets . . . the very poor sections normally tend to be excluded," it [the UN report] says.

While some privatisations have been successful, many companies have faced accusations of profiteering or not meeting pledges to connect poor districts to the mains. British firms have been involved in controversial privatisations in Malaysia, South Africa, Tanzania and Indonesia.

Last week Suez, one of the world's largest water companies, said that it was now impossible for it to work in Latin America. In an interview with the *Guardian*, Jean-Louis Chaussade, the chief executive of Suez Environment, which has major contracts in Argentina, Bolivia and Haiti, said: "We are not a political organisation, but how can we do our job if the political system in countries changes its mind so often? Private funding runs into ideological problems. We need to be more humble. We have to adapt to local realities."

An End to Privatisation

The UN report, which urges private firms to partner local authorities or governments, says the trend of privatisation is now reversing and that local and small-scale water companies are mushrooming. "Their potential to improve water supply remains unexplored . . .There is a need to refocus privatisation. It is high time to bring the government back in," it says.

The report was broadly welcomed by development groups. "Water privatisation in developing countries has failed. Despite this, the UK government and the World Bank insist on supporting it at the expense of the world's poor. Governments and international institutions must . . . invest public money in proven public solutions," said Peter Hardstaff of the World Development Movement in London.

9

Technological Solutions Alone May Not Solve the Water Crisis

Sam Jaffe

About the Author: *Sam Jaffe is a Philadelphia-based associate editor at the* Scientist *magazine, a publication for life science PhD's. He covers issues related to the history, ethics, and philosophy of science, as well as research breakthroughs.*

The planet has enough fresh water for everyone but some countries, such as the United States, use a lot while more than one billion of the world's poorest people don't have enough. This inequitable situation could lead to international conflicts. Global warming is another problem; melting icecaps could cause flooding and erratic rainfall. So far, the world's leaders are talking about the water shortage but no concrete commitments have been made. Water engineer Peter Wilderer argues that the crisis is a poverty and governance problem, not a technology problem. One example is the shrinking of the Dead Sea due to the siphoning off of water from its main feeder, the Jordan River, for agriculture. The World Bank has agreed to build a pipeline to pump water from the Red Sea into the Dead Sea but construction has been held up because of regional violence. Another solution is virtual water, which refers to the amount of water needed to produce goods. Although some countries with water shortages have applied this concept and abandoned an emphasis on agri-

culture, the world is a long way from making this a global policy. Various high technology solutions are being explored but these are all flawed. One idea is trying to induce rainfall by electrical ion generators, but no one is sure this will work. The most popular technological solution is desalination, or taking the salt out of seawater, but this has so far proved to be costly. One process, called multistage flash distillation, is very energy-intensive and another process, reverse osmosis, is more economical but still relies on energy. A third, new technology called capacitative deionization (CD) is expensive now, but relies on very little energy and may eventually provide a cheap solution. Still other researchers are exploring water recycling options. Wilderer, for example, has developed a system that recycles water several times. Even this technology is flawed, however, because it involves complex plumbing systems that could be economically installed only in new construction.

While the planet holds enough fresh water for everyone, it's not distributed well. The average human needs 49 liters [12.9 gallons] of water per day for drinking, cooking, and sanitation. The average US citizen uses 269 liters [70.8 gallons] of water per day. The average inhabitant of the African continent uses 6 liters [1.6 gallons] per day. Meanwhile, more than one billion people, most of them among the world's poorest, don't have access to enough fresh water. That number is expected to double by 2015, and then more than triple by 2050. As a result, more than 76 million people will die over the next 20 years because they can't access enough fresh water, according to the Pacific Institute, Oakland, California.

As water becomes more scarce, it fuels international conflicts. Twenty-two countries depend upon water that flows through river systems that begin in other countries. Many of these are located in flashpoint regions such as the Indian subcontinent, the Middle East, and sub-Saharan Africa. "Water is the one issue," said the late King Hussein of Jordan, "that could drive the nations of this region to war."

Global warming adds another layer of complexity to the equation. If the world's temperature rises, ice caps holding more than half of the world's fresh water will melt, making estuaries flood and rainfall patterns more erratic. Just one example of the dangers inherent in global warming is the melting glaciers of Kazakhstan. Geographer Stephen Harrison of Oxford University says the glaciers have receded so far already that massive rock spills have left rocks clogging up dams throughout Central Asia. "There is a real danger of disastrous dam bursts, hurling rocks and debris on the settlements below."

The World's Response

While such frightening portents have not stirred the world to action, its leaders are certainly talking about the problem. At the United Nations' Millennium Assembly in September 2000, the attendants agreed to cut in half by 2015 the current number of people without enough water. "Other bodies had made similar goals, but this was the first time that all the heads of state of all the nations of the world signed their names to these goals," says Roberto Lenton, chair of the UN [United Nations] Millennium Task Force on Water and Sanitation.

But no blueprints were included with the hopeful declarations. "In order to meet the G8 [a group of industrialized countries including Canada, France, Germany, Italy, Japan, Russia, the United Kingdom, and the United States] goals, we need to construct modern plumbing systems, water sanitation plants and pipelines for 200,000 people every day, from now until 2015," says Peter Wilderer, a civil engineer at the Technical University of Munich, and winner of the 2003 Stockholm Water Prize, the water engineering equivalent of a Nobel [prize]. "Even if we had the several trillion dollars that it would cost, there's no way to organize such a massive project." Wilderer thinks that progress is being made towards the goal, but at only one-half of one percentage point of the necessary rate needed to finish by 2015.

That's why Tony Allan, a geographer at King's College London, urges leaders to understand the real stumbling blocks. "This is a poverty problem and a governance problem," he says. "It's not a technology problem." . . .

The Dying of a Sea

The Dead Sea is, in a word, disappearing. Normally, the Jordan River feeds this body. In the last few decades, however, Israeli and Jordanian farmers have been siphoning water for agricultural use. That's a worldwide trend: More than 80% of the water used in developing nations goes towards agriculture, according to Lenton. Today, the Jordan River is little more than a bubbling brook in the north, reduced to a damp mud bed in the south. By the time it reaches the Dead Sea, it is dry. As a result, nary a drop has refilled the Dead Sea, which, because it's located at Earth's lowest point in the middle of a desert and surrounded by reflective cliffs, evaporates rapidly. The sea's shoreline has already retreated some 24 meters in the past 70 years.

The key is not to import water to thirsty regions, but for those regions to . . . export items that need little water during production, and import water-intensive items.

As the Dead Sea withdraws, aquifers surrounding it are left at a higher level than its surface. Thus, underground water flows into the sea, drying out aquifers that had been untouched for millions of years. The hollow aquifers become brittle and, occasionally, collapse upon themselves, creating sinkholes that dot the region. Much of the farming done at the Ein Gedi kibbutz has been stopped for fear that laborers will be injured by collapsing sinkholes, according to the *Jerusalem Post*.

Experts agree that the Dead Sea is in a deep state of crisis. Once thought to be devoid of life, biologists have recently discovered many types of archaea [a unique, unicellular form of bacteria] that thrive there. One such species, Halobacterium, has become a new model organism for systems biologists, because it can switch between anaerobic [oxygen-free] and aerobic [oxygenated] conditions based on saline levels, according to the Institute for Systems Biology in Seattle. The Dead Sea is also an important stop for one of the world's largest bird migration routes. If it disappears, it could drastically affect wildlife throughout Europe and Africa.

The World Bank has agreed to spend $400 million (US) to build a pipeline from the Red Sea in the south to the Dead Sea. However, the plan hasn't been set in motion, mainly because of fears that regional violence will sabotage it. Meanwhile, every year, the Dead Sea recedes by another one to two meters.

Virtual Water

There are other ways to obtain water that don't involve technology or construction. In 1994, Allan coined the term "virtual water" to mean the amount of water needed to produce goods. The key is not to import water to thirsty regions, but for those regions to alter their economies so that they export items that need little water during production, and import water-intensive items. Already, some countries have turned the term virtual water into a mantra. Israel, for instance, developed a citrus export industry in the first decades of its existence. Oranges and grapefruits can thrive in the Fertile Crescent's sunshine, but they require a lot of irrigation. So now, the Israeli government stresses high technology exports over citrus, and the industry has dried up. Likewise, Jordan has all but abandoned its emphasis on agriculture and favors other sectors such as tourism and heavy industry.

The prospect of changing virtual water from a descriptive device into global policy is not on anyone's agenda, says Margaret Catley-Carlson, chair of Global Water Partnership, a nongovernmental organization. The world is not ready for international oversight of imports and exports to ensure that virtual water policies are intact, she says. "We're a long way from that, but at least the term virtual water has made many people understand that some of our water policies are unsustainable."

High Technology

People elsewhere are turning to high technology to solve water problems. One of the more extreme solutions is a huge steel structure blooming in the desert plains of Jalisco, Mexico. At the base of an enormous web of rods and wires (the footprint covers more than an acre) is an electrical ion [atom with an electrical charge] generator spewing ions into the air. The point of the project, set up by Electrificacion Local de la Atmosfera Terrestre (ELAT), is to cause rain to fall.

The results appear promising, but studies to date lack scientific rigor. Ionogenics, a Boston-based company that licenses ELAT's technology in the United States, claims that over the last three years, 17 generators located throughout six Mexican states caused rainfall to increase by 50% and bean production by more than 60% in the country's central basin region. Of course, correlation is difficult to prove, especially when accurate rainfall statistics for that region have never before been available. In addition, traditional cloud-seeding technologies also have been short on statistical evidence of efficacy. In optimal conditions, seeding clouds with expensive, harsh chemicals such as silver iodide can increase rainfall by 15% at most.

The Holy Grail of water technologists . . . [is] to squeeze the salt out of seawater.

But many are convinced that the plan is working, and Ionogenics is now negotiating for a pilot project in Texas. "We're confident that, if given the chance, we can produce the kinds of results that will satisfy the scientific community that this technology not only works, but works exactly like we say it does," says Judy Lazaro, Ionogenics' vice president of business development. Not all atmospheric scientists share her enthusiasm. "It does not have any physical basis that I can see," says William R. Cotton, a professor of atmospheric sciences at Colorado State University.

Drinking from the Sea

The Holy Grail of water technologists, however, is not producing more rain but using the biggest ponds of all, the oceans. If an affordable way could be found to squeeze the salt out of seawater, the accessibility problem would be officially over. Eighty percent of the world's population lives within 200 kilometers of a coastline. Desalinating seawater is a costly endeavor, mainly because it craves energy. More than 11,000 desalination plants, cleaning billions of liters of water a day, are located throughout the world, primarily in the Persian Gulf. Most of those Gulf-based plants use an older technology called multistage flash distillation, which basically boils the water. The process is extremely energy-intensive, which presents a problem for just about every country except those in the oil-rich Gulf countries.

Reverse osmosis (RO), a more economical technology, uses filters with microscopic pores to strain salt out of water. Thanks to new membrane technologies (which have reduced the cost of such membranes by 80%), RO has become cheaper than flash distillation in the last decade, according to Stamford, Conn.–based Poseidon Resources. However, a great deal of energy is still required to create the pressure needed to push potable water out of the filters. According to the Texas Water Development Board, 1,000 US gallons (equivalent to 3,785 liters) of RO-desalinated seawater costs $2.50, more than double the average price of naturally occurring, fresh water sources. Several large RO plants are being built in the developed world, including Tampa, San Diego, and Singapore. Because most of that price is still linked to energy expenditure, there's little hope that RO will be a primary source of fresh water for the world's poor populations in the future.

Over the last few years, however, a new technology has appeared that provides some hope that desalination might eventually become much cheaper. Developed at the Lawrence Livermore National Laboratory in 1995, capacitative deionization (CD) uses a new substance called carbon aerogel to extract the salt. Aerogel is an extremely porous solid substance consisting of 98% air. Water flows over an aerogel cell that is charged with a 1.2-volt electrical current. As the water moves over the aerogel's surface, salt ions are attracted to the charged cell, affixing themselves inside its pores. Once the aerogel is filled with salt, the polarity is reversed and the salt is flushed. The CD technology has since been leased to a private company, CDT Systems in Dallas. CDT is trying to create a workable mobile system that can be sold to defense contractors or mining operations. The cost of the original aerogel cell at Laurence Livermore was nearly $75,000, but CDT president Dallas Talley claims his company can reduce that figure to $2,000. "And we're still very low on the learning curve on how to manufacture these things cheaply," he says. His company is arranging financing for a new factory to produce large volumes of aerogel cells.

Even at $2,000 for a cell that produces 3,785 liters of desalinated water per day, the cost still exceeds that of reverse osmosis. The reason for excitement about his company's system, says Talley, is that if the capital costs of producing aerogels do come down, then the system becomes very attractive, because energy use is negligible. "The amount of energy we need to desalinate 1,000 gallons of water a day is equivalent to running a 200-watt light bulb."

The ocean's inhabitants would not be harmed by these desalination efforts, researchers say. The larger, and more environmentally dangerous issue, is where to put all that extracted salt. Various plans include diluting it and shipping it to waste sites.

Re-Re-Recycling Water

Development strategists are wary of investing in such expensive technologies in the hope that they eventually will become cost-effective. Some of the more utilitarian water technology research is being done on creating systems that are simple and super-cheap. That's why Wilderer spends his time in his Munich lab monitoring a model sewage system that automatically recycles household water multiple times; the point is that whatever is used returns to the house after it's cleaned. "The cheapest water in the regions that are hardest hit by the water crisis is the water that's already been used," says Wilderer.

[Sewage recycling systems] can be installed only in new construction. Imagine the costs of ripping the walls out of an apartment building to create room for six sets of pipes.

His system involves up to six sets of plumbing pipes, as opposed to the two traditional input and output lines. Water used in the kitchen returns to a neighborhood bioreactor, which filters the water and ferments the kitchen waste to produce methane gas, which is used for energy. Water used in the shower and washing machine goes back to the neighborhood processing center to filter out detergents, a relatively cheap processing method, which also produces industrial chemicals as a byproduct; these can be sold to help pay for the system.

The system has a specially designed toilet that separates body waste into two separate discharge flows. The solid waste is sent through the main sewer to a municipal treatment plant where it composts into fertilizer. The urine is separately processed to produce valuable ammonia fertilizer. "The separation of toilet waste is the key to making this system affordable," Wilderer says. That's because more than 60% of the cost of municipal waste treatment goes towards nitrification and denitrification, chemical processes that essentially remove the urine from solid waste by brute force. By recycling the waste at the source and then separately treating the two waste streams, Wilderer says that his system automatically cuts treatment costs in half.

Nevertheless, the system still has a flaw or two, and even if perfected, it can be installed only in new construction. Imagine the costs of ripping the walls out of an apartment building to create room for six sets of pipes. Some human behavior must be altered in the process, too. Wilderer has designed a test toilet that activates when someone sits on the seat, but he discovered that female subjects produced drastically less urine than males. After trying to fix the seat in the women's bathroom and obtaining the same results, he finally polled the testers and found that about half the women hover over the toilet seat, avoiding direct contact for hygiene reasons. "I didn't know that because I had never been inside a women's bathroom before," says Wilderer. "And it's not the kind of habit people talk about at dinner parties."

10

Better Water Management Is the Key to Solving the Water Crisis

David B. Brooks

About the Author*: David B. Brooks is director of research for Friends of the Earth (FOE) Canada, a charitable, nonprofit environmental organization that is part of Friends of the Earth International, a global network of more than 70 organizations working for a healthy environment and environmental justice.*

There are only two ways to solve the world water crisis: increase supply or moderate demand. Most of the research has been directed at increasing supply but most of the sources of fresh water have already been found and producing fresh water through technologies such as desalinization are expensive and energy-intensive. It is time, therefore, to shift toward managing our demands for water. Management of water demand, however, is complex. Much of the world's fresh water is polluted; water is important for practical as well as environmental and aesthetic purposes; and the value of water depends on many different factors, such as whether is it used for drinking or for agriculture. Some creative programs for water management are beginning to emerge. One idea—setting a price for water—makes sense because it causes people to conserve, but prices must still reflect water quality make sure that everyone has access (regardless of ability to pay) to a minimum quantity necessary for life. There are also technical solutions, such as improving irrigation and collecting rainwater. Yet another option is to allocate water according to the importance of the end use. In Israel, for example, even if farmers are irrigating efficiently, it may be that the whole nation should shift away from agriculture because its water supply is very limited. Still another idea that needs more research is called soft energy paths—various principles designed to promote conservation. Fortunately, unlike the energy crisis of the 1970s when Arab nations cut off much of the world's supply of oil, no country or group of countries is in a position to cut off the supply of water. We simply need to refocus on managing water by increasing research and understanding many of the water management methods that have been around for centuries.

A recent poll of 200 leading scientists from 50 countries identified lack of fresh water as an environmental issue second in importance only to global climate change. One-third of the world's population already experiences severe water scarcity, and another third moderate scarcity. Some 10,000 people die daily from the most common waterborne diseases. And climate change will almost certainly make the situation worse, particularly in the belt that stretches from North Africa to central Asia.

Water Management Is Key

Aside from broad efforts to reduce human impacts on the biosphere by moving towards sustainable development, there are but two ways to provide the peoples of the world with adequate quantities of good quality fresh water: either we increase supply or we moderate demand. Most research is dedicated to increasing supply. But the best and cheapest sources of fresh water have already been tapped. Where does one go when a region is already withdrawing 58 percent of all available water, as in the Middle East, or 41 percent, as in Eastern Europe? A decade ago, the cost of new water supply projects was already two to three times that of existing projects. Today water agencies are turning their attention to desalination, interbasin transfers by pipeline, and shipments by sea. These options are all technically feasible, but they are also capital- and energy-intensive; many have severe ecological impacts and most are politically complex.

It is now time to shift our priorities from finding new sources of supply to managing our demand for water. Water demand management includes greater efficiency in use, reallocation among uses, and changed patterns of use. Though less understood and much less applied than supply management, even preliminary surveys have indicated that the scope for water demand management is large and diverse.

In Canada, which is both rich and wasteful, the wide scope for water demand management should come as no surprise. But how can this be true in regions such as the Middle East, where incomes are low and where water has historically been carefully husbanded? It is true that a Bedouin gets along with as little as five litres [1.32 gallons] per person-day, or less than two cubic metres [439.9 gallons] per year for all purposes. (Each person drinks one cubic metre per year.) However, few people live the Bedouin lifestyle, and the world is increasingly urbanized. Moreover, just as with energy, low income implies low levels of use, but it does not imply efficient use. With lots of low-income people that can cumulate to lots of inefficiently used water. Even countries at the limit of their water availability squander vast amounts of water. Evidently, we need to learn more about water demand management options and how to win them a bigger role in water policy.

Facing the Complexities

Demand management options are too often neglected. One reason for this is the entrenched "supply bias" of traditional water agencies. But this is only part of the story. While demand management may typically be better, it is not obviously easier. Few demand options are energy-intensive or environmentally disruptive but, like supply options, they can be capital-intensive and politically complex. Certainly decision making on demand management initiatives tends to be more dispersed and less amenable to central control than most decision making on supply. And even without the politics, demand management involves a suite of complexities.

First of all, fresh water is not a straightforward physical substance. Some water is a flow resource and some a stock resource. While freshwater stocks (in icefields, lakes and aquifers) are the more obvious supplies, freshwater flows are more crucial for water policy. Moreover, water not only flows, but solid particles and chemicals can move within it. When particles precipitate out, metals such as mercury can adhere to them, and the chemicals can react to form a pollutant far from their original source. Polluted water is always more expensive to handle, and can become useless or hazardous for many purposes.

Second, water serves multiple purposes, most of which are crucial for human life, but not always directly. In addition to its value for immediately practical human uses, water regulates essential ecological processes and life support systems; provides habitat to maintain biological and genetic diversity; and plays less tangible human aesthetic and spiritual roles. Only preliminary work has been done on how to measure the value of these services and to determine how they vary with time and place.

The Value of Water

Even as a narrowly defined economic commodity, water poses difficulties. Water is the text book example of an economic good characterized by a huge gap between marginal price and average price. In practical terms, we will pay a lot for a glass of drinking water but practically nothing for another cubic metre of irrigation water. To complicate things, the value of water depends upon many factors including quality, reliability, timing and location.

The amount of water needed to satisfy thirst is only a few litres per person-day; the amount needed to grow enough food for that person is 50 to 100 times larger. It takes roughly 1000 tonnes of water to produce one tonne of wheat. Thus, the world's major water problem is not water to drink but water to grow food. Two-thirds of all water is used for irrigation; more in some countries. Canada is not typical; less than eight percent of our water is used for irrigation. Nevertheless, irrigation can dominate water use (and politics) in parts of the West; witness the controversy over the Oldman River Dam in Alberta [Canada].

Moreover, water use or withdrawal has to be carefully distinguished from water consumption. Water recycles naturally, and what seems to be waste in one location can be a source of supply for the next, as when water lost because of inefficient irrigation simply flows to adjoining fields. But there are also important losses. The extent of natural recycling within a region ranges from 10 to 80 percent depending upon climate, soil type, land slope and bedrock conditions. And whatever the percentage, return flows will be degraded to one degree or another. They pick up sediment or chemicals, and are of course at a lower elevation.

[Water] prices should be high enough to make consumers think seriously about their water use, but . . . some form of lifeline pricing should be adopted to provide water for basic needs of even the poorest household.

Finally, recycling of water can be enhanced, but challenges are involved here too. Several countries in the Middle East already treat much of their urban wastewater and re-use it for irrigation. Such systems are complex and require fail-safe controls. In villages and remote areas, risks can be minimized by focusing on grey water (wastewater excluding sewage).

Demand management is not simple, but it is clearly possible. Most programs for demand management depend upon some system for pricing water (and, where possible, wastewater), and for seeking out cost-effective improvements in end-use practices. While most current applications fail to address important aspects of the complexities discussed above, more sophisticated and creative options are emerging.

Pricing Water

Putting a price on water is not only . . . economic wisdom, but a fact of life for poor people in many parts of the world. They commonly pay ten times as much per litre for water of questionable quality as do richer people for water of good quality. This is unacceptable. However, it is clear that pricing "works" in the sense that all commercial users of water and most households adjust use in response to price signals. As a result, most analysts see pricing as a necessary but insufficient incentive even for achieving water efficiency, much less equity and sustainability.

Water pricing is difficult. For one thing, only those who treat markets as sacrosanct would deny that everyone has the right to a minimum quantity of water—perhaps 50 litres [13.2 gallons] per day—regardless of ability to pay. Pricing should also reflect water quality. Not all water needs to be potable [suitable for drinking], and recycled water in particular might well be sold for a lower price.

Just as we found for energy after the oil crises of 1973 and 1978, an enormous range of technical fixes can be brought to bear on water demand.

Many analysts want tariffs for water to be designed to encourage conservation, not just to recover costs. Combining this goal with equity implies that prices should be high enough to make consumers think seriously about their water use, but that some form of lifeline pricing should be adapted to provide water for basic needs of even the poorest household. All of these measures depend upon the existence of a more or less sophisticated system for metering water.

Technical Fixes

Just as we found for energy after the oil crises of 1973 and 1978, an enormous range of technical fixes can be brought to bear on water demand. All sorts of publications ranging from newsletters to books are beginning to appear. They show that, in each end-use sector (with the exception of the ecological sector), we could cut the amount of input water needed to provide specified services by factors of two to five with known, cost-effective technologies. The rather conservative International Water Management Institute has concluded that half the additional demand expected over the next 25 years could be met by increasing the effectiveness of irrigation alone, and the rest by small interventions in other sectors.

Other technical fixes depend upon using (commonly relearning) traditional practices. Rooftop rainwater collection is a good example. With rainfall of 400 mm [15.75 inches] a year, it is quite possible to collect enough water from the roof of a single-family home to cover potable water needs for a year. The real trick is to store the water in such a way that it stays clean.

Rain can also be collected in the countryside and directed to a field where crops are grown. Two millennia ago, the Nabateans, a desert people who lived in what is now southern Israel and Jordan, and who built the rock city of Petra, used water harvesting not only to feed themselves but also to supply passing caravans. Rainwater harvesting works best where, some years, there is almost enough rain for agriculture and many years when erratic rainfall means no crop at all (regions of 100 to 500 mm [3.94 to 19.68 inches] of rain per year). Today, these old techniques are being improved by use of GPS

[Global Positioning System] methods, laser-guided leveling of fields, and analytical models to optimize among key variables.

Reallocation Among Sectors

Technical fixes focus on end-use efficiency. However, in many cases the end-use itself must be questioned. Even if a farm, for example, is irrigating efficiently, one must still ask whether it should be irrigating at all. Perhaps the farmer should plant less water-intensive crops, or move to rain-fed agriculture. Perhaps the whole nation should shift away from agriculture. Israeli farms using drip irrigation can be 95 percent efficient in terms of getting water to the roots of plants, but with agriculture accounting for only a few percent of the nation's GNP [Gross National Product], it does not make sense to devote over 60 percent of a limited water supply to this one low-value end-use.

Because of the many subsidies for water supply systems, and the role water commonly plays in local and national politics, it can be very difficult to determine which economic sectors should get water, and at what price. In many countries, agriculture serves as the reserve sector for water. Farmers pay less for irrigation water but are cut back when supplies are short.

Soft Path Options

Pricing and technical fixes may be the common stuff of demand management today, but they rely on conventional concepts and tools. A more ambitious and radical perspective is modeled on the highly successful approach to energy analysis dubbed soft energy paths. Soft paths are based on a number of principles designed to promote conservation. For example, one principle is to match the quality of the resource supplied to the quality required by the end use. It is almost as important to conserve the quality of water as to conserve quantity. We only need small quantities of potable (high quality) water but vast amounts of irrigation (low quality) water.

So far, soft paths for water have received only initial analysis. However, we can already see lessons analogous to those from energy, which suggests that this approach has great promise for the future, which is when many (perhaps all) countries will need it.

No country is in a position to cut off the supply of water, and no group of nations has oligopoly power.

Three Needs

We appear to be in a situation for water that resembles the urgent energy situation created by the oil crises in the 1970s [in which several Mideast countries cut off oil exports to western nations, including the United States]. The analogy is happily more apt from an analytical than a political point of view. No country is in a position to cut off the supply of water, and no group of nations has oligopoly power. However, current practices for supply and delivery of fresh water are outmoded. Getting consensus on the following three points would help a great deal:

- Whether the issue is global climate change or local conflict resolution, success will come less from greater water supply than from water demand management.

- Although demand management is our best option for dealing with water problems, it is the least understood. We need to initiate active research and information programs.

- Finally, though there is ample scope for technical research and information, technology is not the big problem. Most of the methods and tools have been around for centuries.

We now need to focus on the economics of demand management, on social and cultural impacts, on behavioural and gender aspects, and on the institutions that can creatively manage and accelerate the adoption process—in the broadest sense of the word, on governance of water demand management.

11

Supply and Demand Strategies Must Be Applied to Alleviate Water Problems

Center for Strategic and International Studies

About the Author: *The Center for Strategic and International Studies (CSIS) is a bipartisan, nonprofit organization that seeks to advance global security by providing strategic insights and practical policy solutions to decision makers. CSIS conducts research and analysis and develops policy initiatives on various issues, including the water crisis.*

Decades of research on the problems of fresh water shortages have provided an extensive list of options for addressing the world water crisis. Neither technological solutions nor policy changes alone will be effective, but together, they can be applied to augment water supply, reduce demand, and improve water management. Supply can be augmented by a variety of both large- and small-scale strategies. Large-scale infrastructure projects such as dams, for example, will be necessary in some regions, while some of the poorer, more rural areas of the world will need to seek cheaper, community-based solutions or inexpensive, easy-to-use technologies. Demand can also be reduced by a mixture of technology and policy solutions. Technologies such as recycling are available as well as policy ideas such as shifting water tariffs or providing tax incentives for water reduction. The most significant way to reduce demand, however, is to reduce the water used in agriculture, through improved irriga-

tion systems and eliminating agricultural water subsidies. Finally, it will be important to improve water management from the local to the international level, in order to allocate available water to necessary uses—drinking, industry, agriculture, and the environment. To accomplish these goals, funding will have to be increased from the current level of about $75 billion a year to twice that amount. This means that the private sector will have to remain involved, even though recent attempts to privatize water utilities (by selling them to private companies) in developing countries have largely failed. By creating enforceable regulations, strengthening oversight, and inviting public participation, the world should be able to provide a way for corporations, nongovernmental organizations, and governments to work together to solve the water crisis.

After decades of research and projects focused on alleviating freshwater problems across the planet, the global community has reached an unprecedented level of understanding of the intricacies of the global water challenge and has developed an extensive tool box for addressing these issues. Indeed, many of the solutions to the web of interrelated problems will come from a combination of policy and technological approaches. Taken alone, neither policy breakthroughs nor technological innovations can solve regional and global water-scarcity issues, but together they offer a potentially powerful synergy. These synergistic solutions can be applied to three broadly defined strategies: augment supply; reduce demand; and improve management. In all three of these strategies, one single observation reigns true—there is no silver bullet, no one-size-fits-all solution.

Augment Supply

Augmenting water supplies by both expanding access and improving quality will be a key part of meeting global water challenges. Water supply augmentation is a determinant of success, whether we consider reaching the Millennium Development Goals [eight goals set by the United Nation to address world poverty] of halving the number of people without access to safe drinking water or simply satisfying the growing and competing demands of industry, agriculture, energy, and the environment. Strategies to expand access and water treatment can and should be conducted at both a large and small scale.

Large-scale infrastructure projects that store, convey, and otherwise manage the natural water supply play a significant role in economic development. According to the World Commission on Dams, approximately 30 to 40 percent of the world's irrigated croplands, producing 12 to 16 percent of the world's food, rely on dams to provide water. Without developed water storage and management infrastructure, areas of the world with highly variable rainfalls are more susceptible to economic fluctuation.

For example, the World Bank estimates that a series of floods and droughts in Kenya between 1997 and 1998 cost the country the equivalent of 22 percent of its GDP [Gross Domestic Product] in either damages or lost crops. Without dams, the problem is one of too much and too little water. Building large-scale infrastructure, however, requires a strong and open governance framework in order to attract financial support, to help develop a sustainable plan for development and management, and to protect the environment. Good governance has been and will continue to be a requirement for the development of large-scale infrastructure in the future.

Large-scale infrastructure or even connections to preexisting infrastructure are usually not an option for the poorest communities across the world, both urban and rural. Easily accessible and safe drinking water are in high demand. In many cases, community-based solutions that incorporate the input, ingenuity, and leadership of local people have proven to be highly sustainable. Such frameworks have been successfully applied to projects from expanding pipes into urban slums to encouraging safe water storage practices in homes.

Improving efficiencies in agriculture . . . represents the most significant potential reduction in global water withdrawal.

Inexpensive, easy-to-use technologies are another key ingredient to successful solutions, particularly for water treatment and safe water storage. Some element of social change or social marketing is also typically involved. The U.S. Centers for Disease Control and Prevention developed the "Safe Water System" consisting of three steps: (1) point-of-use water treatment; (2) safe water storage; and (3) behavior change. Field trials conducted in South America, Africa, and Central Asia have proven to reduce the risk of diarrhea, the number one killer of children worldwide, by 44 to 85 percent. The long-term sustainability and strategies for scaling up the Safe Water System and other community-based approaches remain unclear.

Reduce Demand

Reducing demand also relies on a mixture of technology and policy-based solutions. Certainly, technologies exist to reduce global water withdrawals significantly, but current regulations, subsidies, and market structures do not provide adequate incentives for ready adoption of these technologies. Recycling techniques, low-flow appliances, dry-cooling units, leak detection, and improved pipes and valves could all significantly reduce the amount of water withdrawn for municipal and industrial uses. Initiating widespread adoption of such technologies in the developed world could be as simple as shifting water tariffs, providing certain tax incentives, regulating new construction, or even a public awareness campaign.

Improving efficiencies in agriculture, however, represents the most significant potential reduction in global water withdrawal. Shifting from conventional and wasteful surface irrigation to drip and low-loss sprinkler technologies is proven to increase overall water productivity from 25 to over 200 percent for crops as diverse as bananas, cotton, sugar cane, sweet potatoes, and food grains. Despite the potential water efficiency improvements, only about 1 percent of irrigated farmland worldwide currently uses precision irrigation. Domestic and industrial users often pay over 100 times as much per unit as agricultural users. Thus, water subsidies provide few incentives for farmers to adopt more efficient practices or grow less water-intensive crops.

Finally, improved water management strategies and structures from the local to the international level will go a long way in providing safe drinking water to the world's poor while also ensuring enough water for industry, agriculture, and the environment. Many experts and policymakers have pointed to privatization as a way to improve efficiencies and service at the local level. However, good governance, firm regulatory frameworks, and strong institutions are a necessary foundation for privatization to work and sustainable management practices to be achieved.

Funding Needs

Of the $75 billion spent annually on water services, about 70 percent comes from government, 20 percent from the private sector ranging from small water vendors to private municipal and metropolitan utilities, 13 percent from international donors, and the remainder from the international private sector. Estimates show that current spending will need to double in order to meet current and future demand. With this magnitude of need, the private sector will have to be involved in the expansion of water services through financial backing and expanding technical capacity. Recent attempts to privatize utilities in the developing world have failed due to significant public backlash or unfulfilled contract obligations by the local municipalities. Gordon Binder of Aqua International Partners stated at a conference at CSIS in February 2005, "The business model hasn't worked for international operators in developing countries. Cost recovery is a laudable yet elusive goal."

Enforceable regulatory frameworks, stronger institutions, and more participatory processes will provide the necessary environment for corporations, nongovernmental organizations, and governments to capitalize on their core competencies and maximize positive results. Such frameworks and structures are also necessary to improve management of water supplies that cross international boundaries.

12

Worldwide Efforts Are Necessary to Prevent a World Water Crisis

UN/WWAP (United Nations/World Water Assessment Programme)

About the Author: *The World Water Assessment Programme is part of the United Nations Educational, Cultural and Scientific Organization (UNESCO) and is designed to provide information related to global freshwater issues. Every three years, it publishes the United Nations World Water Development Report (WWDR), a comprehensive review that gives an overall picture of the state of the world's freshwater resources and aims to provide decision-makers with the tools to implement sustainable use of our water.*

A billion people, or one-sixth of the total world population, live in extreme poverty, subject to disease, hunger, thirst, lack of housing, exploitation, and a low quality of life. The availability of clean water is central to alleviating poverty, and providing the water needed to feed the world's growing population and meet other demands for water from industry and the environment is one of the great challenges of this century. Today, in many parts of the world, water quantity is decreasing and water quality is increasing. Yet the lack of clean water is often caused not by water shortages, but by social and political factors. The key to solving the water crisis and meeting the United Nations' Millenium Development Goals for alleviating world poverty, therefore, is better governance and better water management. Environmental sustainability is also a key to these goals. A holistic, ecological approach, which considers all related problems and is tailored to local conditions, is necessary. Solving water problems will also take private investment, which in turn will depend on improving local governance. Finally, finding solutions to the water crisis will require international and national cooperation; poor countries must make policy changes and improve their governments, while industrialized countries must provide development aid and technical assistance. Already, there has been some progress: Poverty is lessening; countries such as China, India, and Brazil have set up improved water governance and delivery systems; and financing is improving. The United Nations recommends several strategies, one of which is for all levels of society—individuals, localities, national governments, and the international community—to assume responsibility for taking action on the world water crisis.

A pproximately 1 billion people worldwide, one-sixth of the total world population, live in extreme poverty, sickness, hunger, thirst, destitution and marginalization. The lifestyle of the extreme poor is based on subsistence living. Many poor families occupy land over which they have no formal legal rights—in a squatter community or slum, or farming on marginal lands owned by others with limited access to reliable water. Women and girls in particular often have the least entitlement to household or family assets. Very poor households are rarely connected to infrastructure, such as piped water, sanitation and electricity supply. The payment structure for many utility services (water, electricity), with their up-front connection and monthly consumption charges, are often too expensive for the poor.

All of this creates an ideal environment for disease transmission, vulnerability to loss of housing and possessions and, overall, a low quality of life. Poor families face difficulties accumulating surpluses—food and financial—and find it difficult to maintain consumption when their incomes are interrupted or their crops fail. In addition, limited or non-enforcement of laws, regulations and procedures concerning legal and political rights, environmental health and protection, occupational health and safety, crime prevention and safeguarding from exploitation and discrimination, are common. Unbridled competition from richer farmers and industrial concerns for water, productive land and fisheries, often put the poor at a serious disadvantage. It is also often very difficult for the poor to assert their rights and needs so as to receive a fair entitlement to public goods and services.

Water and Poverty

Water is central to alleviating poverty. Some 13 percent of the world's population—over 800 million people—do not have enough food and water to live healthy and productive lives. Providing the water needed to feed a growing population and balancing this with all the other demands on water is one of the great challenges of this century. Providing water for environmental flows and industry will tax water resources even more. Extending water services to the 1.1 billion un-served with improved water supply and the 2.6 billion lacking improved sanitation will enlarge the challenge even further. Confronting water-related disease—including malaria, which causes 300 to 500 million episodes of sickness and 1.6 to 2.5 million deaths each year—must be done. In many parts of the world, available water quantity is decreasing and quality is worsening.

Water insufficiency is primarily caused by inefficient supply rather than by water shortages. Water insufficiency is often due to mismanagement, corruption, lack of appropriate institutions, bureaucratic inertia and a shortage of investment in both human capacity and physical infrastructure. Water shortages and increasing pollution are socially and politically induced challenges. These can be addressed by modifying water demand and usage through increased awareness, education and water policy reforms. The water crisis is thus increasingly about how we govern access to and control over water resources and their benefits.

Solutions to Water Problems

Many of the solutions to water problems lie in better governance. Water is central to promoting socio-economic development, protecting the environment, and achieving the Millennium Development Goals (MDGs [eight goals set by the United Nations for alleviating world poverty]). Yet, few lower-income countries include water as a key feature of their national planning and budgets. Mismanagement of water is widespread, characterized by lack of integration, sectoral approaches, and institutional resistance to change by large public agencies in a context of increasing competition. Only a minority of local authorities and water associations have the resources needed to carry out the responsibilities delegated from central governments.

Social and economic resilience is the key to sustaining development and meeting societal goals. The UN Millennium Project [a United Nations project for alleviating world poverty] has stated that long-term success in meeting the MDGs depends on environmental sustainability. Without it, any gains will be short-lived and inequitable. Part of the problem is the very modest political effort devoted to sustainable development, compared with global economic growth.

A Holistic Approach

Water problems and challenges are connected and should be addressed in a holistic manner. The various water issues are interdependent and greater wisdom is required in the allocation and management of water resources. A flexible approach is essential at both strategic and local levels. The answer to this, including meeting the MDGs, lies in a holistic, ecosystem-based approach known as Integrated Water Resources Management (IWRM). IWRM has to be tailored to prevailing socio-economic conditions. Local circumstances, however, can put obstacles in its way:

- lack of proper coordination of management activities
- lack of appropriate management tools
- inability to integrate water resources policies
- institutional fragmentation
- insufficiently trained or qualified manpower
- shortfalls in funding
- inadequate public awareness
- limited involvement by communities, NGOs and the private sector.

Because of these obstacles and other difficulties, very few countries have met the Johannesburg Plan of Implementation (JPOI) target stating that IWRM should be incorporated into national water resources plans by the end of 2005.

Reliable data is essential for IWRM. A holistic approach to water management requires knowledge of the different systems involved: not just hydrological, but socio-economic, political, institutional and financial. However, data on almost every subject relevant to water issues is often lacking and may be inconsistent, unreliable or incomplete. Collection of data in itself is insufficient. It must be synthesized, analysed and compared to other sources. . . .

The water sector needs greater investment. Lack of reliable information and indicators has contributed to serious underinvestment and inadequate donor aid to the sector. Private investors are discouraged because they perceive the sector as presenting higher risks, and longer and lower returns on investment than other sectors. Both public and private sector investors are also deterred by inadequate governance. Recent information, however, shows that investments in the water sector have become increasingly cost-effective. Rapidly deployable interventions targeted at the poor including improved household water treatment and storage are one example. For the irrigation sector, drip irrigation and treadle pumps are two cost-effective ways in which access to small-scale water technology can be provided to poor farmers.

Lower-income countries are tasked with delivering promised policy changes and improvements to government; the industrialized countries must follow through with their long-standing commitments to increase [development assistance].

Greater transparency, accountability and stakeholder involvement is needed. One of the biggest roadblocks to achieving the MDGs is lack of investment by external donors. However, lack of good governance is often a constraint to such financing. This can be addressed by encouraging transparency and accountability. This necessitates greater stakeholder involvement at all levels of government and the involvement of major groups and the private sector.

International and National Cooperation

International and national cooperation is required to meet the MDGs related to poverty alleviation and water. While it is imperative that as much action as possible to meet the MDGs must be initiated within countries themselves, there is also a moral obligation that the richer countries be prepared to share their wealth to meet the goals. The lower-income countries are tasked with delivering promised policy changes and improvements to governance; the industrialized countries must follow through with their long-standing commitments to increase ODA [Official Development Assistance] and technical assistance. It should be noted, however, that even if the

MDGs are achieved there will still be a significant segment of society remaining unserved—and these will probably be the poorest of the poor.

The world today has the wealth and tools to do what is needed.

There are many instances of improvement. The first step to better governance is awareness, followed by commitment and stakeholder involvement. Indicator development and case study work both show that progress is being made. Economic development can and does work in many parts of the world. The scale of extreme poverty is lessening, both in terms of the total numbers affected and as a proportion of the total world population. The rapidly growing lower-income countries—Brazil, China and India—have set up a wide range of initiatives for improved water governance and water service delivery challenges, which could be adapted by other countries. The growth in microfinance has the potential to provide essential capital for the extension of water service provision, through a much-enhanced availability of funds to the very poor, and to contribute also to lessening their insecurity. However, funding for microfinance houses must go beyond its traditional sources such as governments, aid agencies and charities. The cost of operations must also be decreased, because microfinance as presently organized is very labour-intensive.

Without access to secure water supplies, development will stall and the MDG targets will fall short. The Millennium Project has made clear that the world today has the wealth and tools to do what is needed. With determination and political will, the levels of international cooperation agreed in the Millennium Declaration, and re-confirmed at the 2005 UN World Summit, water sector reform and the MDGs can be achieved.

Recommendations for Action

- To appreciate the context within which water issues must be approached.

- To recognize that the various issues of water are inter-related—and with growing demand and, in general, decreasing supply, competition between uses and users is increasing, requiring greater wisdom in allocation of the resource.

- To appreciate the variety of circumstance—solutions have to be tailored to situations.

- To understand that water moves within natural limits—but that these do not usually correspond to the administrative units within which societies organize themselves.

- To improve basic data through research. Greater knowledge and understanding are prerequisites for better management of all the systems involved.

- To focus on governance.

- To anticipate and adapt to changing circumstance.

- To all assume responsibility for action: There is a need for responsible action and involvement at all levels of society. Individuals at community level should be encouraged and given the means to take responsibility for their own problems. Likewise, at local and national levels, governments must take their share of responsibility. At international levels, responsibility must be taken to set goals and targets towards which the world should strive, and to assess the global situations with a view to sharing knowledge.

Organizations to Contact

The editors have compiled the following list of organizations concerned with the issues debated in this book. The descriptions are derived from materials provided by the organizations. All have publications or information available for interested readers. The list was compiled on the date of publication of the present volume; the information provided here may change. Be aware that many organizations take several weeks or longer to respond to inquiries, so allow as much time as possible.

Global Water
3600 S. Harbor Blvd., # 514, Oxnard, CA   93035
(805) 985-3057 • Fax: (805) 985-3688
e-mail: info@globalwater.org
Web site: www.globalwater.org/index.htm

Global Water is an international nonprofit, nongovernmental organization dedicated to helping to provide clean drinking water for developing countries. The organization provides technical assistance, water supply equipment, and volunteers to help poor countries develop safe and effective water supply programs around the world.

International Water Management Institute (IWMI)
P. O. Box 2075, Colombo
   Sri Lanka
+94-11 2787404, 2784080 • Fax: +94-11 2786854
e-mail: iwmi@cgiar.org
Web site: www.iwmi.cgiar.org/index.htm

The International Water Management Institute (IWMI) is a nonprofit scientific organization funded by the Consultative Group on International Agricultural Research (CGIAR). IWMI concentrates on water and related land management challenges faced by poor rural communities.

Natural Resources Defense Council (NRDC)
40 West 20th Street, New York, NY   10011
(212) 727-2700 • Fax: (212) 727-1773
e-mail: nrdcinfo@nrdc.org
Web site: www.nrdc.org/water/default.asp

The Natural Resources Defense Council (NRDC) is a U.S.-based environmental action organization that uses law, science, and the support of 1.2 million members and online activists to protect the planet's wildlife and wild places and to ensure a safe and healthy environment for all living things. Its Web site includes a section on Clean Water and Oceans with numerous news items, reports, and links about drinking water, pollution, oceans, and conservation and restoration of water resources.

National Water Resources Association (NWRA)
3800 North Fairfax Drive, Suite 4, Arlington, VA   22203
(703) 524-1544 • Fax: (703) 524-1548
e-mail: nwra@nwra.org
Web site: www.nwra.org

The National Water Resources Association (NWRA) is a non-profit federation of state organizations whose membership includes rural water districts, municipal water entities, commercial companies and individuals. The NWRA is concerned with the appropriate management, conservation, and use of water and land resources in the United States.

U.S. Geological Survey (USGS), Water Resources of the United States
USGS National Center, Reston, VA   20192
1-888-275-8747
Web site: http://water.usgs.gov/

Water Resources is one of four science disciplines of the U.S. Geological Survey (USGS). Its mission is to provide reliable, impartial, timely information about U.S. water resources.

The World Bank, Water Supply & Sanitation
1818 H Street NW, Washington, DC   20433
(202) 473-1000 • Fax: (202) 477-6391
Web site: http://web.worldbank.org/

The World Bank is an international organization that provides
loans, grants, and technical assistance to developing countries
around the world to help them reduce poverty and improve
education, health, infrastructure, communications, and many
other critical areas of national development. Its Web site contains news and information about global water issues under
the topic, Water Supply and Sanitation.

World Water Council (WWC)
Espace Gaymard, 2-4 place d'Arvieux, Marseille   13002
   France
+33 4 91 99 41 00 • Fax: +33 4 91 99 41 01
Web site: www.worldwatercouncil.org/about.htm

The World Water Council (WWC) was established in 1996 in
response to increasing concern from the global community
about world water issues. Its mission is to promote awareness,
build political commitment, and trigger action on critical water issues at all levels to facilitate the efficient management
and use of water on an environmentally sustainable basis.

UNESCO World Water Assessment Programme
7, place de Fontenoy, Paris 07 SP   75352
   France
+33 (0)1 45 68 10 00 • Fax: +33 (0)1 45 67 16 90
e-mail: waterportal@unesco.org
Web site: www.unesco.org/water/wwap

The World Water Assessment Programme is part of the United
Nations Educational, Cultural and Scientific Organization
(UNESCO) and is designed to provide information related to
global freshwater issues. Every three years, it publishes the
United Nations World Water Development Report (WWDR),

113

a comprehensive review that gives an overall picture of the state of the world's freshwater resources and aims to provide decision makers with the tools to implement sustainable use of our water.

Bibliography

Books

Ronald C. Griffin — *Water Resource Economics: The Analysis of Scarcity, Policies, and Projects.* Cambridge, MA: MIT Press, 2006.

Constance Elizabeth Hunt — *Thirsty Planet: Strategies for Sustainable Water Management.* New York: Zed Books, 2004.

Jun Ma — *China's Water Crisis.* Norwalk, CT: EastBridge, 2004.

Bernadette McDonald and Douglas Jehl, eds. — *Whose Water Is It?: The Unquenchable Thirst of a Water-Hungry World.* Washington, DC: National Geographic, 2003.

Kendra Okonski, ed. — *The Water Revolution: Practical Solutions to Water Scarcity.* London: International Policy, 2006.

Fred Pierce — *Keepers of the Spring: Reclaiming Our Water in an Age of Globalization.* Washington, DC: Island Press, 2004.

Fred Pierce — *When Rivers Run Dry: Water, the Defining Crisis of the Twenty-first Century.* Boston: Beacon Press, 2006.

Mark W. Rosegrant — *World Water and Food to 2025: Dealing With Scarcity.* Washington, DC: International Food Policy Research Institute, 2002.

Fredrik Segerfeldt   *Water for Sale: How Business and the Market Can Resolve the World's Water Crisis.* Washington, DC: Cato Institute, 2005.

Zmarak Shalizi   *Addressing China's Growing Water Shortages and Associated Social and Environmental Consequences.* Washington, DC: World Bank, Development Research Group, Infrastructure and Environment Team, 2006.

United States Congress, Committee on International Relations   *Water Scarcity in the Middle East: Regional Cooperation as a Mechanism Toward Peace: Hearing Before the Committee on International Relations House of Representatives, One Hundred Eighth Congress, second session, May 5, 2004.* Washington, DC: U.S. Government Printing Office, 2004.

Diane Raines Ward   *Water Wars: Drought, Flood, Folly, and the Politics of Thirst.* New York: Riverhead Books, 2002.

Linda Whiteford and Scott Whiteford   *Globalization, Water, & Health: Resource Management in Times of Scarcity.* Santa Fe, NM: School of American Research Press, 2005.

Periodicals

Ed Ayres   "Desalination Getting Serious," *World Watch*, September–October 2003.

Muhammad Saleem Ayub and Waqar Murtaza Butt — "Nuclear Desalination: Harnessing the Seas for Development of Coastal Areas of Pakistan," *International Journal of Nuclear Desalination*, May 3, 2005.

Edward B. Barbier — "Water and Economic Growth," *Economic Record*, March 2004.

David Barkin — "Mexico City's Water Crisis," *NACLA Report on the Americas*, July–August 2004.

Theresa Bray — "Water Crisis Looms Unless We Understand Freshwater Cycles," *Cosmos Online*, August 25, 2006.

Nicholas L. Cain and Peter H. Gleick — "The Global Water Crisis," *Issues in Science and Technology*, Summer 2005.

Rory Clarke — "Introduction: Water Crisis? Humankind's Relationship With Water and, Indeed, Its Struggles Around It, Will Grow in Importance in the Next Century," *OECD Observer*, March 2003.

Clifton Coles — "The Growing Water Crisis: Given the Growing Scarcity of Water, It's Time to Change Water Policies Worldwide," *Futurist*, September–October 2003.

Gayle Ehrenman — "U.S. Seeks to Avert Western Water Crisis," *Mechanical Engineering–CIME*, June 2003.

Engineer	"Water Crisis: Running Dry," June 27, 2005.
Environment	"Water Crisis in the Canadian Prairies," June 2006.
Futurist	"Africa's Hidden Water," September–October 2002.
Rakesh Kalshian	"Mainstream News Reporting Ignores Critical Water Issues: In India, 'Reportage on This Complex Subject Has Regressed to Its Earlier Character—Unsophisticated and Immature,'" *Nieman Reports*, Spring 2005.
Gary D. Libecap	"The Myth of Owens Valley: Los Angeles's 'Theft' Offers Positive Lessons for Water Markets," *Regulation*, Summer 2005.
Ronald MacDonald	"Providing the World With Clean Water: Remains a Complex Problem, But Time Is Running Out," *British Medical Journal*, December 20, 2003.
Chandra A. Madramootoo and Colleen N. Robson	"Today's Water Crisis—A Global Vision," *Journal of Eastern Township Studies*, Fall 2003.
Diane Martindale	"Waste Not, Want Not: In the World's Arid Regions, Even Sewage Water Cannot Be Thrown Away," *Scientific American*, February 2001.

Jason J. Morrissette and Douglas A. Borer	"Where Oil and Water Do Mix: Environmental Scarcity and Future Conflict in the Middle East and North Africa," *Parameters*, Winter 2004.
New Scientist	"Africa's Water Crisis Deepens," March 11, 2006.
New Scientist	"To Feed Itself Africa Must Capture More Rainwater," August 28, 2004.
Fred Pearce	"Asian Farmers Suck the Continent Dry: The World Is On the Verge of a Water Crisis As People Fight Over Ever Dwindling Supplies, Experts Told the Stockholm Water Symposium," *New Scientist*, August 28, 2004.
Fred Pearce	"Russia Revives Epic River Plan: Countries in Central Asia Are Facing a Water Crisis. Is the Solution to Revive a Huge Soviet-era Engineering Project and Turn the Flow of Siberia's Major Rivers South?," *New Scientist*, February 7, 2004.
Fred Pearce	"Safe Water Remains a Mirage," *New Scientist*, March 29, 2003.
Vandana Shiva	"Now Monsanto Is After Our Water," *Ecologist*, August–September 1999.
Laurie A. Shuster	"Water Access Reaching Crisis Level," *Civil Engineering*, April 2003.
John M. Swomley	"When Blue Becomes Gold," *Humanist*, September 2000.

Melissa Taylor   "States Face Water Wars," *State Government News*, September 2003.

Maria de los   "Analysing Rationing Policies:
Angeles Garcia   Drought and Its Effects on Urban
Valinas   Users' Welfare," *Applied Economics*, May 10, 2006.

E. Weinthal, A.   "The Water Crisis in the Gaza Strip:
Vengosh, A.   Prospects for Resolution," *Ground*
Marei, A.   *Water*, September–October 2005.
Gutierrez, and W.
Kloppmann

Web sites

BBC, World Water Crisis (http.//news.bbc.co.uk/hi/english/ static/in_depth/world/2000/world_water_crisis/). A British Web site providing information about some of the world's water flashpoints.

Global Policy Forum (www.globalpolicy.org/security/natres/ waterindex.htm). A Web site run by a no-profit, nongovernmental organization that contains analysis and articles relating to global water policies.

Nature Publishing Group (www.nature.com/nature/focus/ water/index.html). A science Web site with an analysis of the global water crisis that includes a collection of news, features, and interactive graphics.

U.N. Environment Program UNEP.Net Freshwater Portal (http://freshwater.unep.net/). A United Nations Web site with information and links about various global water issues.

U.S. Environmental Protection Agency (EPA) (www.epa.gov/ safewater/dwinfo/ca.htm). A U.S. government Web site with information about the sources and safety of tap water in the United States.

World Water Day: March 22 (www.worldwaterday2006.org/). This is a United Nations Web site set up for events and information related to "World Water Day," March 22, a day designated by the UN General Assembly to draw international attention to the critical lack of clean, safe drinking water worldwide.

Index

A

Aerogel, 84
Afghanistan, 45
Africa
    cooperation in, 50–51
    daily per capita use in, 33, 78
    infrastructure deficiencies in, 16
    irrigation with wastewater in, 18
    population/water resource balance in, 13
    savannahs in, 22–23
    undeveloped water resources in, 39–40
Agriculture
    amount of use of, 15, 16–17, 23, 43, 91
    contamination by, 29
    in developing countries, 80
    growing population's need for, 22
    increased production of, needed in developing countries, 15
    increasing efficiencies in, 101
    low-value end-uses of, 94
    raise cost of water to, 32
    virtual water calculations of, 81
    See also Irrigation
Allan, Tony, 80, 81
Angola, 51
Aquifers
    contamination of, 28
    depletion of, 9–10, 80
    disputes over regional, 8
    storage and recovery of, 18

Asia
    irrigation with wastewater in, 18
    population/water resource balance in, 13
    water-related disasters in, 38–39
Australia, 23, 27–28

B

Bangladesh, 15
Bedouins, 89
Binder, Gordon, 102
Bottled water, 55
Brazil, 23
Brooks, David B., 87
Bulk water, 58–60

C

Cambodia, 50
Campo, Max, 39
Canada, 91
Capacitative deionization (CD), 84
Carbon aerogel, 84
Carius, Alexander, 47
Catchments, 29–30
Catley-Carlson, Margaret, 81–82
CDT Systems, 84
Center for Strategic and International Studies, 97
Central Intelligence Agency (CIA, U.S.), 43
Cerrados, 23
Chalecki, Elizabeth L., 54
Chaussade, Jean-Louis, 75
Chemical contamination, 17

China
    future scarcity in, 44
    water footprints of, 33
    water tables dropping in,
      15–16
Climate change effects, 7, 13, 35–
  36, 79
Colorado River, 16–17
Community-base programs, 99–
  100
Conservation
    encouraging, through pricing,
      67
    privatization and, 64
    promoting, with soft paths,
      94–95
    technologies, 93–94, 100
Consultative Group on Interna-
  tional Agricultural Research, 20
Consumption *vs.* use, 91
Contamination
    aquifers and, 28
    chemical, 17
    in developed countries, 29
    must be reduced, 32
    salinity and, 27, 28, 29
Cotton, William R., 83
Culture and water, 36–37, 57
Custom-Built Solutions For Inter-
  national Disputes (Dellapenna),
  45–46

D

Dabelko, Geoffrey D., 47
Dams, 33, 99
Dead Sea, 80–81
Deister, Ane, 16, 17, 18
Dellapenna, Joseph W., 45–46
Demand management
    difficulties, 89–90
    impact of, 96

    moderating demand with, 88,
      100–101
    questioning end-use as part
      of, 94
    research, 95
    supply bias and, 89
Desalinization technologies, 17,
  83–85
Developed countries
    areas of scarcity and, 12, 16–
      17, 27–28
    common problems in, 28–30
    daily per capita use in, 32
    have obligation to developing
      countries, 108
    privatization has benefited, 75
    quality is primary concern in,
      14
Developing countries
    agriculture in, 80
    daily per capita use in, 32–33
    developed countries have obli-
      gation to, 108
    funding projects in, 40
    government improvements in,
      109
    population growth in, 14–15
    privatization has not ben-
      efited, 75–76
    rate of water-related diseases
      in, 14
    supply is primary concern in,
      14
Dickie, Phil, 25
Disasters, water-related
    droughts as, 12, 16, 99
    extent of, 36, 38
    floods as, 31, 99
    preventing, 38–39
Diseases
    poverty factors and, 104
    water-related, 14, 53, 88, 105

Drinkable water, access to, 13–14, 35

Droughts, 12, 16, 99

E

Earth, surface water, 12
Economic good, water as, 55, 60
    controversy about, 70–71
    determining value of, 90, 92–93
    international recognition of, 57
    See also Prices
Ecosystem services, 30
Egypt, 9, 23
Ehrenman, Gayle, 11
Electrificacion Local de la Atmosfera Terrestre (ELAT), 82–83
Endocrine disruptors, 29
Environment
    damaged, 29–30, 33, 80–81
    measures to protect, 18, 31
    privatization negatively effects, 64, 66
Environment News Service, 34
Equitable utilization, 46
Ethiopia, 9
Euphrates River, 9, 45
Europe, 27, 32, 88

F

Fauchon, Lïoc, 37
Floods, 31, 99
Freshwater
    limited supply of, 26–27
    stocks *vs.* flows, 90
    unavailable, 12–13
Funding, 38, 101–102, 107–108, 109

G

General Agreement on Tariffs and Trade (GATT), 58–59
Gleick, Peter H., 54
"Global Patterns" (CIA), 43
Global warming effects, 7, 13, 35–36, 79
Globalization, 58–60
Government
    improvements in, will solve many water issues, 106
    infrastructure development and, 40, 99
    investment in water sector and, 107, 108
    progress in improving, 109
    regulation and oversight of privatization, 68–69, 101–102
    subsidies, 94
    water responsibilities, 62, 65–66
Groundwater supply, 15–16, 28, 44
    See also Aquifers
Guardian (newspaper), 75

H

Hardstaff, Peter, 75–76
Harrison, Stephen, 79
Hashimoto, Ryutaro, 38
Headwater Diversion Plan (Jordan and Syria), 7–8
Household water, 85–86
Hurricane Katrina, 39
Hussein (king of Jordan), 78

I

India, 44, 50
Infrastructure
    African, 16

damaged in developed countries, 30
environmental damage by, 33
governance requirements for, 99
investments in, 40–41
repairing, 32
Integrated Water Resources Management (IWRM), 106–107
Interdependence, water increases, 48, 49–53
International Conference on Water and Environment, 57
International Decade for Action Water for Life, 37
Investment, 40–41, 101–102, 107–108, 109
Ionogenics, 82–83
Iraq, 9, 44–45
Irrigation
    water amount used by, 15, 91
    dams, 99
    technologies, 18–19, 101, 108
    using collected rainwater, 93–94
    using wastewater, 18
Israel
    agriculture in, 81, 94
    Jordan River diversion and, 7–8, 43
    Jordan River talks and, 50
Italy, 23

J

Jaffe, Sam, 77
Jaime, Cristóbal, 37–38
Japan, 28, 32, 33
Jerusalem Post (newspaper), 80
Jordan
    agriculture in, 81
    River diversion, 7–8, 43
    River talks, 50

Jordan River
    Dead Sea and, 80–81

K

Kashmir, 44
Kazakhstan, 79
Kenya, 99
Kim Huk Su, 38, 39
Kramer, Annika, 47
Kupchinsky, Roman, 42

L

Laos, 50
Lazaro, Judy, 82–83
Lebanon, 7–8
Lenton, Roberto, 79

M

Malaria, 14
Matsuura, Koichiro, 12, 36–37
Mauritania, 12
Mekong Committee, 50
Methyl-tertiary-butyl ether (MTBE), 17
Mexico, 41
Microfinance, 109
Middle East
    Euphrates River in, 9, 45
    Jordan River in, 7–8, 43, 80–81
    non-military water disputes in, 7–10, 44–45
    percent of available water used in, 88
    water wars, 7, 8, 43, 50, 78
Molden, David, 22, 24
Molina, Mario, 35–36
Mozambique, 51
Multistage flash distillation, 83

N

National Water Carrier project (Israel), 7
Natural recycling, 91
The New Water Politics Of The Middle East *(Strategic Review)*, 45
Nile River, 9
North America, 32, 39
North American Free Trade Agreement (NAFTA), 58–59

O

Oceans. *See* Desalinization

P

Pacific region, 38–39
Pakistan, 44, 50
Palestinians, 8
Peace, water increases chances of, 48, 49–53
Perchlorate, 17
Pollution
    amount of, deposited daily, 13
    in Europe, 27
    privatization and, 64
    See also Salinity
Population
    near river basins, 22, 49
    percent of, affected by scarcity, 21, 22
    water resource balance and, 13
Population growth
    agricultural needs and, 22
    demands of, 8, 16
    developing countries and, 14–15
Poseidon Resources, 83–84
Postel, Sandra, 15–16

Potable water, access to, 13–14, 35
Poverty
    extent of, 104
    lessening of extreme, 109
    relationship of water to, 22, 105–106
    and water subsidies for poor, 66, 67
Prices
    according to types of users, 101
    difficulties in determining, 90–91, 92–93
    encouraging conservation with, 67
    and equitable return for private companies, 68
    privatization may increase, 62–63
    subsidized, 66, 67
    vs. true costs, 30, 32
Privatization
    dangers of, 62–65
    government regulation and oversight of, 68–69, 101–102
    nations benefiting from, 75–76
    opposition to, 40–41, 61–62, 74
    principles and standards for, 56, 66–69
    social values and, 70–71
    types of, 60–61
    water as economic good and, 55
Public water agencies, 60–61, 62

Q

Quality of water
    in developed countries, 14
    ensuring, 68
    matching, to end-use, 94
    protecting, 64

R

Rainfall, 82–83, 93–94
Rate structures. *See* Prices
Recycling and reuse
 of household water, 85–86
 importance of, 18
 natural, 91
Religious significance of water, 57
Reservoir capacity, 28
Reverse osmosis (RO), 83–84
Reyes, Rachel, 54
Rijsberman, Frank, 21, 22, 23
Riparian nations, 46, 50, 51–53
River basins, 22, 49

S

Salinity, 27, 28, 29
Sanitation, 14, 35
Saudi Arabia, 9–10
Savannahs, 22–23
Scarcity
 areas of persistent, 16–17, 23, 27–28
 causes of, 7, 8
 extent of, 88
 forecasts, 13, 43–45
 is opportunity for cooperation, 50–53
 percent of population affected by, 21, 22
 supply management causes much, 105–106
Seawater. *See* Desalinization
Serageldin, Ismail, 48
Sewage systems, 85–86
Sharon, Ariel, 43
Sierra, Kathy, 40
Six-Day War (1967), 7, 8, 43
Social good, water as, 57, 70
Soft path options, 94–95

South Africa, 50–51
Southeast Anatolia Project (GAP, Turkey), 9, 44–45
Southern Africa Development Community (SADC), 51
Strategic Review (journal), 45
Strock, Carl, 39
Subsidies, 66, 67, 94
Sudan, 9
Suez Environment, 74, 75
Supply bias, 89
Supply management
 augmenting, 98–100
 causes much scarcity, 105–106
 See also Technologies
Syria
 Euphrates River and, 9
 GAP and, 44–45
 Jordan River diversion and, 7–8

T

Talley, Dallas, 84
Technologies
 are not solution, 79–80
 conservation, 93–94, 100
 desalinization, 17, 83–85
 increasing rainfall with, 82–83
 irrigation, 18–19, 101, 108
Thailand, 23, 50
Thames Water, 74
Trade in bulk water, 58–60
Tropical storms, 39
Turkey, 9, 44–45
Turral, Hugh, 12, 14, 15, 18–19

U

United Nations, 12
United Nations/World Water Assessment Programme (UN/WWAP), 103

United States
    daily per capita use in, 78
    desalinization in, 17–18,
        83–84
    salinity contamination in, 27
    scarcity in, 12, 16–17, 27
    water-related disasters in, 39
Urban areas, 15

V

Vidal, John, 73
Vietnam, 50
Virtual water, 33, 81–82

W

Wastewater, 18, 30
Water crisis
    defining, 14
    is overstated, 48
Water disputes (non-military)
    in developed countries, 29
    in Middle East, 8–10, 44–45
Water footprints, 33
Water for People, Water for Life
    (UN), 12
Water for Schools initiative, 37
Water Resources Development in
    Africa: Challenges Response and
    Prospective, 39–40
Water use
    agricultural, 23, 43, 91

    agriculture *vs.* urban, 15,
        16–17
    vs. consumption, 91
    daily per capita, 8, 32–33, 78,
        89
    domestic, 15
    extent of available, 88
    low-value end, 94
Water wars
    areas of possible future, 44–46
    within countries, 49
    Middle East, 7, 8, 43, 50, 78
West Bank Mountain Aquifer, 8
Wilderer, Peter, 79, 85–86
Wolf, Aaron T., 47
Wolff, Gary, 54
World Bank
    Dead Sea project, 81
    funding in developing coun-
        tries, 40
    privatization and, 61, 74–75
World Commission on Dams, 33
World Trade Organization
    (WTO), 58–59
World Water Development Report
    (UN), 12

Y

Yarmuk River, 8

Z

Zimbabwe, 12